GRASSROOTS
ADMINISTRATION

WITHDRAWN

O9-BUD-942

GRASSROOTS ADMINISTRATION

A HANDBOOK FOR STAFF AND DIRECTORS OF SMALL COMMUNITY-BASED SOCIAL-SERVICE AGENCIES

ROBERT L. CLIFTON
METROPOLITAN STATE COLLEGE

ALAN M. DAHMS
METROPOLITAN STATE COLLEGE

WITHDRAWN

BROOKS/COLE PUBLISHING COMPANY
MONTEREY, CALIFORNIA
A DIVISION OF WADSWORTH, INC.

© 1980 by Wadsworth, Inc., Belmont, California 94002. All rights reserved. No part of this book may be reproduced, stored in a retrieval system, or transcribed, in any form or by any means—electronic, mechanical, photocopying, recording, or otherwise—without the prior written permission of the publisher, Brooks/Cole Publishing Company, Monterey, California 93940, a division of Wadsworth, Inc.

Printed in the United States of America

10 9 8 7 6 5 4 3 2 1

Library of Congress Cataloging in Publication Data

Clifton, Robert L.
    Grassroots administration.

    Bibliography: p. 176
    Includes index.
    1. Social work administration.   I. Dahms, Alan M.,
joint author. II. Title.
HV41.C546   361.7   79-26640
ISBN 0-8185-0345-9

Project Development Editor: *Ray Kingman*
Production Editor: *Robert Rowland*
Interior and Cover Design: *Ruth Scott*
Illustrations: *Ann Geiger, The Design Company*
                Appendix C: Pat Kelly
Typesetting: *Donna Sharp*

361.7
C 639g

PREFACE

The recent emergence of small social-service agencies is an interesting and significant social development. These agencies, which often rely heavily on volunteer support, are meeting human needs that would otherwise go unmet. Many people no longer expect civil servants and large governmental programs to respond quickly and flexibly to social needs. Instead, people from all walks of life are attempting to meet those needs in a variety of ways.

Grassroots Administration is designed to provide information on a broad range of functions that are important to the effective administration of small, community-based social-service programs. Although we emphasize practical skills, such as the ability to obtain funds, justify their use, solicit and organize volunteers, design a brochure, and write a quarterly report, we have also included theoretical models and suggestions for further reading.

This book is written for students enrolled in the growing number of programs that prepare people for professional positions in community service as well as for church workers, service-club members, volunteer organizers, members of neighborhood associations, and participants in community service and development programs. Anyone interested in a "how to do it" approach to meeting the demands of a difficult administrative role can find useful ideas in this text.

We chose the topics presented here by asking members of small agencies and programs what functions were most critical to the effective administration of their particular services. The material was then tested and applied in actual administrative situations.

Following an introduction to small community-service programs, we present topics in five parts. Part I explores the planning, funding, and evaluation of programs. Part II deals with communication skills. In order to maintain and expand popular support for programs, you need to communicate your progress and your needs. Tips are included on writing a variety of reports and using the media effectively. Part III explores the effective use of volunteer support systems. Part IV examines the politics of agency survival: lobbying, conflict among agencies, and decision-making techniques are discussed. Part V explores the dynamics of staff development. In the appendixes, we provide suggestions for further reading, primary sources of foundation publications, and the basics of graphic design.

Any book is a product of a distinctly human process. We wish that we could thank everyone whose ideas, guidance, and inspiration nurtured us in this effort. Thanks go to our contributors, and to Ray Kingman and Claire Verduin

35598

of Brooks/Cole Publishing Company, whose patience, professional guidance, and friendship were a constant influence. Thanks also go to Dan Cowley of Wayne Community College, Mele Koneya of the University of Nebraska, Dorothy Kostriken of Monterey Peninsula College, Cherry Michelman of Springfield Technical Community College, Keith Miller of the University of Wyoming, and Pat Thornton of Community Hospital of the Monterey Peninsula for their reviews of the original manuscript of this book. Special thanks go to Mavis Knopp and Bettye Ruettimann of Metropolitan State College, Denver, who helped us in thousands of small ways. To Heather Clifton and Polli Dahms we can only say thank you for allowing us the time and personal space we needed to complete this project. Your support has been the real key to our success.

Robert L. Clifton
Alan M. Dahms

CONTENTS

INTRODUCTION   1

    What Are Community-Based Social-Service Agencies?   2
    Services Provided by Small Community-Based Agencies   2
    Funding   5
    Who Runs Community-Based Social Service Agencies?   6
    Clientele of Small Social-Service Agencies   7
    How Small Social-Service Agencies Are Initiated
       and Developed   8
    What Can You Do?   9

**PART ONE   PLANNING, FUNDING, AND EVALUATING
           PROGRAMS   11**

CHAPTER ONE   Program and Resource Development   13

    Three Basic Concepts Regarding Program Development   15
    Step 1:   Developing a Good Idea and Overcoming
       White-Paper Shock   16
    Step 2:   Testing and Researching   17
    Step 3:   Initial Contact   19
    Step 4:   Meeting the Potential Funding Source   19

Step 5:   Writing the Formal Proposal   19
Summary   24

CHAPTER TWO   How to Develop Goals and Procedures   25

The Importance of Goals and Objectives   27
Goals and Objectives   27
Evaluation   28
Why Are Goals and Procedures Necessary?   28
The Difference Between Agency Goals and Project Goals   29
Goals and Procedures: How Do They Differ?   30
Writing Goal and Procedure Statements   31
Summary   32
Suggested References   32

**CHAPTER THREE   Creative Fund Raising: The Key To
                     Agency Survival   33**

Planning and Research   35
Soliciting Large Contributions   37
Soliciting Medium Contributions   38
Soliciting Small Contributions   40
Ideas and Techniques for Limited Fund Raising   40
Summary   45
Suggested References   46

CHAPTER FOUR   Evaluating Social-Service Programs   47

Introduction   49
What is Evaluation?   50
Why Evaluate Programs?   51
Who Should Evaluate Programs   52
When Should Programs Be Evaluated?   52
How Are Programs Evaluated?   53
Four Essential Elements of Evaluation   56
The Cost of Program Evaluation   60
Summary   61
Suggested References   61

PART TWO   COMMUNICATIONS   63

CHAPTER FIVE   Writing As a Communication Tool   65

Introduction   67
Choosing the Best Form of Written Communication   68

Informal Reports   68
Steps to Writing an Effective Report   73
Writing the First Draft of Your Report   76
Checking the Effectiveness of Your Report   77
Revising and Rewriting Your Report   78
Proofreading Your Report   79
Formalizing Your Report: Preliminary and
    Supplementary Sections   79
Summary   82
Suggested References   83

CHAPTER SIX   How To Develop An Agency Newsletter   85

The Purpose of a Newsletter   87
Materials Needed to Produce a Newsletter   88
Producing a Newsletter   88
Putting Your Newsletter to Bed   89
How to Build the Circulation of Your Newsletter   93
How to Evaluate Your Newsletter   94
Summary   94
Suggested References   94

CHAPTER SEVEN   Using Press Releases and
                  The Broadcast Media   97

Introduction   99
Planning Your Publicity   99
Reaching the Public   99
Three Channels of Communication   100
Word of Mouth   100
Newspapers   100
The Broadcast Media   102
Summary   107
Suggested References   108

PART THREE   VOLUNTEER SUPPORT SYSTEMS   109

CHAPTER EIGHT   Effective Volunteer Programs   111

Attitudes Toward Volunteers   113
The Director of Volunteers   114
The Functions of the Director   116
Summary   122

CHAPTER NINE   The Role of Governing Boards in
                    Community-Service Agencies   **123**

The Philosophy Underlying the Creation
   of Governing Boards   125
Community Representation   125
The Role of the Governing Board of Directors   126
Planning Policy   127
Legal Responsibilities of Governing Boards   129
Dealing with the Realities   129
Summary   129
Suggested References   130

**PART FOUR   THE INTERNAL AND EXTERNAL POLITICS
                OF AGENCY SURVIVAL   131**

CHAPTER TEN   The Lobbying Process and the
                    Community-Service Agency   **133**

What is a Lobbyist?   135
Know the Tax Rules   136
Preparing Your Lobbying Effort   137
Establishing Your Agency's "Presence"   137
Approaching a Legislator   138
Testifying in Committee   138
Statehouse Etiquette   139
Lobbying: A Year-Round Job   139
Summary   139

CHAPTER ELEVEN   Conflict Resolution: A Problem-Solving
                       Approach for Community-Service Agencies   **141**

What is Conflict?   143
Assessing the System   144
Identifying the Conflict   144
Setting Goals   145
Generating Plans of Action   145
Critiquing and Prioritizing Plans of Action   146
Selecting and Implementing a Plan of Action   146
Evaluating Results and Revising Techniques   147
Summary   148
Suggested References   148

PART FIVE   STAFF AND LEADERSHIP DEVELOPMENT   149

CHAPTER TWELVE   Organizational Influences, Individual Behavior, and Styles of Leadership   151

Internal Influences   153
External Influences   153
Individual Behavior Patterns   156
Identifying and Choosing a Style of Leadership   157
Summary   158
Suggested References   159

CHAPTER THIRTEEN   Emotional Survival   161

Introduction   163
Thriving Skills   164
Summary   171
Suggested References   171

Afterword   175
Appendix A: Bibliography   176
Appendix B: Primary Sources of Foundation Publications   179
Appendix C: Graphics Made Simple   184
Index   192

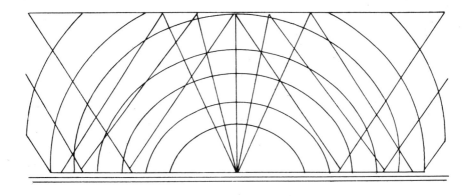

THE
EDITORS

INTRODUCTION

WHAT ARE COMMUNITY-BASED SOCIAL-SERVICE AGENCIES?

Finding the most effective and least expensive solutions to problems such as drug and alcohol abuse, juvenile delinquency, illiteracy, poverty, and the plight of the aged is one of the most important tasks facing us today. During the past 15 years, thousands of small, nonprofit, community-based agencies have been established in response to these and other social problems. Community-based social-service agencies are those whose scope of operation is focused on the immediate community or on specific issues within a community and whose principal function is to meet a specific social or human-service need. These grassroots organizations are usually effective, because they are able to take risks, adjust to societal changes, and provide opportunities for people willing to engage in one-to-one relationships with clients.

The staffs of these agencies usually consist of a director, an assistant director or project coordinator, a secretary (usually part-time), and a volunteer support system. Volunteers perform highly specialized functions that require experience and skills as well as odd jobs that require no formal training. Annual operating funds, derived from local contributions, federal grants, and other sources, may run as high as $250,000 but usually range between $30,000 and $90,000. The director or administrator of such an agency must be adept at writing funding proposals, promoting public relations, managing volunteers, assuming leadership, making decisions, and resolving conflicts.

In one survey, we contacted 150 social-service agencies and asked for information concerning their operations. These agencies ranged in size from very small, experimental projects with annual operating budgets of less than $1000 to large, multiservice organizations with budgets of several million dollars. We examined the information we received from the agencies that met the criteria of small, community-based social-service programs identified earlier and discovered some similarities in the services offered by these agencies, their funding procedures, their personnel, and the clients they served. Although our sample wasn't exhaustive, we believe that the similarities and characteristics we discovered provide insights into the administration and operation of individual agencies. The information we gathered concerning the personnel and clientele of the agencies we examined is presented in Table 1.

SERVICES PROVIDED BY SMALL COMMUNITY-BASED AGENCIES

Referral. Referral is a valuable service for people in need of help and for those who are intimidated by complex bureaucratic systems. Some referral

TABLE 1

Personnel and Clientele of Community-Based Social Service Agencies in the Denver Metropolitan Area (1977)

Groups [a]	Average Full-Time Staff	Average Part-Time Staff	Agencies Using Volunteers	Agencies Not Using Volunteers	Average Number of Volunteers	Ratio of Volunteers To Staff	Total Number of Clients	Average Number of Clients
I Less than $25,000	1.4	1.9	15	2	32.9	14.0	11,205	659
II $25,000 to $99,999	3.4	2.04	24	2	99.5	22.5	181,802	6,992
III $100,000 to $249,000	9.55	4.0	17	3	163.6	14.2	482,100	24,105
All Groups	4.65	2.62	56	7	88.6	14.8	675,107	10,715

[a] Programs were grouped according to size of annual budgets.

agencies are prepared to help almost anyone who has a problem, while others deal with a very specific clientele. These latter agencies are staffed by people who are familiar with the particular problems of their clients and the specific resources they require.

Education. Education includes a wide range of services, such as job training, development of consumer skills, remedial education, special training for the physically or mentally disadvantaged, and the establishment of alternative schools. Educational programs may involve long-term training, such as the "Right to Read" program, or they may involve only a few sessions.

Job Placement. Agencies that focus on job placement and training view employment as an important component in a comprehensive program designed to serve the needs of their clients.

Advocacy and Outreach. Advocacy and outreach are two of the most common functions of community-service organizations. It is the responsibility of every human-service agency to make its clientele and the public aware of the services it can provide and to demonstrate the need for those services. There are also agencies whose primary function is to call attention to social problems and advocate solutions. They lobby, publicize issues, and try to bring specific problems to the public's attention. The American Civil Liberties Union, the National Association of Neighborhoods, and the Children's Defense Fund are examples of such agencies. Other groups, such as those established for the retarded, are advocates for a more specific client population.

A number of agencies offer what might be called *quality-of-life supplements.* Examples include materials and labor provided for the renovation of old houses, special recreational equipment, or a stock of canned food.

Crisis aid is another example of outreach. One "store-front" operation included in our survey deals solely with victims of crime and family tragedy, maintaining a 24-hour "victim line" and "family-disturbance" line. This agency also engages in outreach programs to increase community awareness. Advocacy services for victims in hospitals and institutions provide short-term counseling as well as the option of more extensive counseling when it is required.

Some programs provide residential accommodations for their clients. Religious organizations that offer temporary lodging to those who require it have been joined by small agencies that provide a similar service. One program in our survey, for example, provides residential accommodations and child care for low-income, single-parent families.

Counseling is another service provided by many programs. Some agencies act as crisis-intervention centers, offering immediate, short-term counseling. Other agencies provide both short-term and long-term counseling. For example, various "substance-abuse" programs offer detoxification, out-patient, and non-medical therapy for alcoholics. Most multiservice organizations list counseling as one of their services.

Advocacy and outreach inevitably involve research and the collection of data. Decision makers respond most effectively when presented with accurate information about the extent of existing needs and the important factors that influence solutions. For example, an agency that helps in the reconstruction of homes needs accurate information concerning the extent of disrepair, building codes, cost of materials, zoning restrictions, and so on.

Outreach programs that provide one-to-one helping relationships perform what we call *personal-sharing functions.* Big Brothers, Big Sisters, and Partners are examples of such programs. Through the relationships established in these programs, clients come to realize that someone cares enough to invest time and emotional commitment in an effort to help them.

A number of agencies under the heading of *advocacy and outreach* perform the important function of organizing: they supply other programs and agencies with staff members, support funds, and technical expertise. Local branches of the Mennonite Urban Ministry and the Involvement Corps are examples of agencies that fulfill a "brokering" role, matching up contributing individuals and services with specific programs and recipients.

FUNDING

Most of the funds for the agencies studied in our survey came from federal and private sources (see Table 2). In our survey, Group I was composed of agencies with budgets of less than $25,000. Group II was composed of agencies with budgets of over $25,000 and less than $100,000. Group III included all agencies with budgets of over $100,000 but less than $250,000.

Several facts become apparent when one compares the funding of the three different groups. First, no large program uses state or local funding alone as a significant source of money. Second, small agencies (agencies with budgets of less than $25,000) are less likely to be federally funded. Finally, the largest programs (Group III) are least likely to be funded primarily from private sources.

Budget size varies within each group. A few of the agencies in the first group reported that their budgets were under $1000, but their figures probably represented actual cash used for operations rather than their total available resources. If an organization has a budget of $1000 or less, it is likely that office space and the use of a phone or other utilities are not included as part of the operating budget. The average budget of the agencies in Group I was $12,318; however, if hidden resources had been taken into account, this figure would have been several thousand dollars higher. Most of the small agencies in our survey had actual operating budgets of between $10,000 and $20,000.

TABLE 2

Funding Sources of Community-Based Social-Service Agencies

	Group I: Less than $25,000	Group II: $25,000 to $99,999	Group III: $100,000 to $249,999	All Groups
Agencies primarily or totally funded by a federal source	2	10	7	19
Agencies primarily or totally funded by a state source	0	0	0	0
Agencies primarily or totally funded by a local source	1	3	0	4
Agencies primarily or totally funded by a private source	7	9	3	19
Agencies funded by two or more primary sources	4	11	10	25
Average budget	$12,318	$50,649	$160,450	$76,198

In our survey, we found that, although agencies with budgets of $25,000 to $99,999 offer the same types of services that small agencies offer, they typically serve more clients and maintain a wider range of services within each of their programs.

The largest agencies examined in our survey—those with budgets of $100,000 to $249,999—offered many of the services provided by smaller organizations. However, the larger the organization, the more closely it resembled large, permanently established governmental social-service agencies.

WHO RUNS COMMUNITY-BASED SOCIAL-SERVICE AGENCIES?

Since there are few academic programs specifically designed to prepare individuals for administrative positions in social-service agencies, most administrators and directors of such agencies gain their competence through on-the-job training. The majority of administrators who hold college degrees studied one of the social sciences—psychology, sociology, political science, and so on. These are the disciplines that have traditionally been most concerned with human needs and social issues. Although these individuals may have a strong desire to alleviate human suffering and resolve social problems, they frequently lack the specific skills and knowledge they need to be effective administrators of small community-based social-service agencies. These agencies require administrative leadership from individuals who have the ability to prepare budget requests, develop funding proposals, evaluate programs, manage public relations, write reports, diagram systems that clarify objectives, and design methods of assessment.

The following job advertisement, which appeared in a major newspaper, is an indication of the current situation.

> Coordinator for Community Action Program. Must have B.A. degree in Psychology, Sociology, Political Science, Public Administration or related field. Experience desired in writing funding proposals, community organizing, program assessment, public relations and volunteer management.

The academic disciplines mentioned in the advertisement don't relate directly to the specific tasks performed by a coordinator for a community-action program. Small social-service programs and agencies lack the financial resources needed to provide individual positions for public relations, goal evaluation, volunteer coordination, and so on. These tasks are usually performed by a director, an assistant director, and a part-time secretary.

Business programs in colleges and universities haven't recognized the special administrative needs of small social-service agencies. As one professor of business said, "Personnel management is personnel management. It doesn't matter whether you are dealing with U.S. Steel, a large food market, or a community mental-health program." Statements such as this ignore the sensitive climate of a small agency, where interpersonal skills are essential and authority must be earned.

The data from our study indicated that volunteers are used in most social-service programs, regardless of the agency's size, and that the size (based on operating budget) of the agency does not significantly alter the ratio of volunteers to paid staff.

The data also showed that the average number of clients served was proportionately much greater for large agencies than for small ones. It should be noted, however, that this statistic does not indicate anything about the quality or nature of the services.

CLIENTELE OF SMALL SOCIAL-SERVICE AGENCIES

Since small social-service agencies are more flexible and less complex than large governmental organizations, they are usually able to respond more effectively to individual needs. Moreover, the "nonestablishment" character of small agencies allows their staff members to form relationships with clients that are based on trust. For example, K. L. Berry, Research Director of a small organization that helps former prisoners find jobs, describes the general attitude of his clientele in the following way.

> Many of our clients are quite hostile to the government in general and suspicious of governmental employees who are supposed to be concerned with their welfare. Since we are not a government agency, and since some of our people are ex-offenders themselves, we have a much better chance of establishing trust and getting them to commit themselves to really trying to work with the program.

Small social-service agencies provide assistance to a wide range of individuals: elderly people who have limited financial resources, teenagers "on the run," veterans involved with drug abuse, family members coping with divorce, recently widowed individuals struggling to deal with their loss, and countless others. These individuals could become social casualties if inexpensive, effective, and *immediately available* help and support were not made available.

It's difficult to determine the exact number of individuals being served by small agencies. For example, an individual who is referred to one agency by another becomes a statistic in the records of both agencies. Regardless of this lack of precision, however, it's obvious that a need does exist for the services these small agencies provide. Over 675,000 people were indicated as being served by the 63 organizations examined in our survey. Even allowing for the fact that one individual may be counted as a client with several agencies, this is an impressive figure. Moreover, it should be noted that the agencies included in our survey represent only a small portion of the 2000 agencies that exist in the metropolitan area we examined.

HOW SMALL SOCIAL-SERVICE AGENCIES ARE INITIATED AND DEVELOPED

An agency or program often begins with a creative idea. Someone might say "If only we could find a way to help." Soon thereafter, planning sessions are held, funds are obtained, volunteers are recruited, and a new program or agency is created, providing a proving ground for the new idea. In many ways, creating a small social-service agency is similar to starting a small business: it requires dedicated, hard-working individuals who understand the necessary elements of successful operation, as well as leaders who can deal with staffing limitations and the need for involved persons to do many things well with a minimum of formal training.

A life cycle seems to exist with regard to small social-service organizations. During the initial phase of the development of these agencies, an idea is conceived, funding is obtained, and the delivery of services begins. In the intermediate stage, programs are modified to better meet actual needs. In the final stage, the agency becomes permanently established or is absorbed by a larger agency.

WHAT CAN YOU DO?

The fact that you are reading this book indicates that you are interested in small community-based social-service agencies and the functions they perform. Once you've mastered the skills presented here, you will be able to help solve a variety of social problems. This will not be an easy venture; however, your reward will be a sense of personal worth and satisfaction in knowing that you are part of a process that directly affects individual lives.

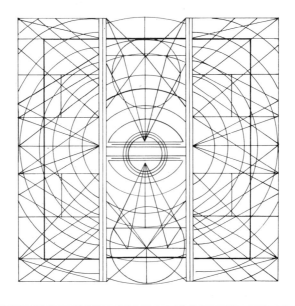

PLANNING,
FUNDING,
AND EVALUATING
PROGRAMS

PART ONE

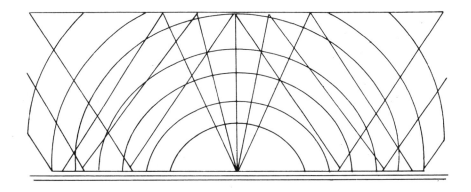

PROGRAM AND RESOURCE DEVELOPMENT

Joe Cavanaugh

CHAPTER 1

"The future of small, community-based, social-service agencies will be determined by the ability of these programs to successfully compete for grants and resources for program development. I can think of no other single activity more critical for a director of a program to occupy his or her energy with than developing skills in grant writing."

Joe Cavanaugh is the Coordinator of Community Development and Neighborhood Planning for the city of Boulder, Colorado. He is a former Peace Corps Volunteer and VISTA staff member. He is currently involved in grassroots politics and community organization.

The development and planning stage of any social-service agency is the key to that agency's eventual success. In this chapter, we briefly summarize the basic strategy involved in program and resource development and explain how to prepare program proposals.

We will consider the following questions in this chapter:

What are the basic concepts of program development?
How do you overcome "white-paper shock"?
How do you locate a funding source?
What do you do after you've located a funding source?
What are the important elements of a funding proposal?

THREE BASIC CONCEPTS REGARDING PROGRAM DEVELOPMENT

1. *Program development is an art, not a science.* There isn't one specific formula that can be used as guide to developing a successful program. When individuals conceptualize and fit the pieces of their programs together, they function as artists. Their individual personalities and unique perspectives shape their programs and, to a considerable extent, determine their success. Imagination and industry are the most important determinants of success.

2. *People give money to people.* Those who solicit funds for small social-service agencies cannot depend solely on well-written and carefully documented proposals. There are other factors that are equally critical in determining the ultimate success of their efforts. They need to establish a relationship and some credibility with the individuals who are responsible for allocating funds. A 30 minute meeting in which you request advice on developing better proposal documents is a legitimate, useful, and flattering way to introduce yourself to such people. There is no need to be coy. Simply tell the person that you would like him or her to become acquainted with the work of your agency.

3. *The local "bake-sale" approach to fund raising is a legitimate and critical method of obtaining resources.* In many cases, this approach may be more appropriate than a formal grant proposal. Organizations often spend valuable time drafting ambitious proposals for expensive, large-scale programs that have a low probability of success. Program goals that might be realized on a limited scale are then displaced by the pursuit of a grand but illusory concept. Administrators of community-based agencies should determine to what extent their organizational goals can be met without major funding. There is always some risk that a large, well financed agency may lose sight of a program's original objectives.

With these three strategic principles in mind, we will now examine the stages of program development.

STEP 1: DEVELOPING A GOOD IDEA AND OVERCOMING WHITE-PAPER SHOCK

Program development begins with a good idea. In order to convey an idea to others, you need to write a concise statement of your concept. If you find it difficult to start this task (as most of us do), the following steps will help you to overcome *"white-paper shock."*

1. Preparation. Assemble the following materials in a quiet, peaceful environment: a long sheet of unruled paper, a pen or pencil, a comfortable chair, and a table or desk.

2. Brainstorming. Begin promptly. Think about your idea. List any other ideas that might affect or relate to your basic thought. Quickly write down anything that comes to mind. Don't take time to judge your thoughts: let your mind fly. You are now brainstorming. You need to get as many thoughts as possible down on paper, so don't worry about spelling, neatness, or grammar at this point. When you have filled the page, your task for this phase is completed. You should relax and let your subconscious work. In two or three days, you should be ready for the next phase of Step 1.

3. Organization. Return to your paper. Look the page over carefully and choose the one idea you consider to be the best; this idea will become your primary idea. Don't choose too quickly or start automatically at the top of the page and work your way sequentially to the bottom. When you are confident that you've selected the best idea, write a large number 1 next to it in the margin. Now read through the list again and identify those thoughts that support your primary idea and number these 1a, 1b, and so on. Then read through the ideas again, pick out the second-best idea, and write a large number 2 next to it in the margin. Read through the ideas again and identify those items that support this second-best idea. (Each supporting item may be used for more than one major idea.) Repeat this process for your third idea and the items that support it. Look at the remaining points to see whether there is anything that could support one of your three ideas. When nothing usable remains, cross out the remaining material. You have sucessfully completed your task for this phase. Within a day or so, you should be ready for the next phase of Step 1.

4. Writing. Read and think through your list again, beginning with the primary idea and all of the items that support it. Then write each major idea in narrative form. Since you are writing a rough draft, you shouldn't be critical of your grammar, spelling, or sentence structure. When you have finished this phase, put the material aside for at least a few hours and allow your thoughts to "germinate" in your mind. Imagine how your rough draft will read after you've completed your editing.

5. Editing. This is the final phase of Step 1. You are now ready to combine your idea with the total perspective of your program. Although you might use very little of the original material in your final draft, you now have a comprehensive understanding of your idea. With this understanding, you can draw up a list of the following items to be included in a one-page statement or summary of your proposal.

1. The *history of your organization.* This brief history puts your group in perspective for the funding source. You need to include only the date on which your group was organized, its goal(s), and any recent successes in areas that pertain to your proposal.

2. A statement of the *needs* your proposal will address. This should be brief but specific, and it should be documented as much as possible. (Simple referral to a reliable source is all that is required for documentation. For example, you might say "According to the Federal Report on . . .")

3. A statement of the *specific objectives* of your program. For example, you might say "Our program will provide 2000 child-care days if funded at the proposed level for one year."

4. A *budget* that spells out the total dollar amount your program requires. This should consist of one or two lines that show your program's total cost, including the projected cost for personnel, major expenses, and any anticipated matching funds.

5. A *timetable* that specifies a starting date for your program and projects its operation three to five years into the future.

STEP 2: TESTING AND RESEARCHING

When you have your one-page statement in hand, you are ready to test the acceptance and feasibility of your idea and research possible sources of support.

Phase 1: sharing and endorsement. In the first phase of Step 2, you present the one-page statement of your proposed program to the staff and governing board of your agency. This phase is completed when the governing body or board has formally voted to endorse the one-page statement you've prepared. Their endorsement authorizes you to seek funding for the program with the formal support of your agency. If you are not part of an existing agency or program, you should form and obtain the support of an ad hoc advisory group.

Phase 2: exposing your idea to other professionals in your field. In exposing your idea to other professionals in your field, you have an opportunity to see your proposal from their point of view. This phase is very important: it gives you the benefit of others' experience, brings you up-to-date on current activity in your field, and helps to prevent costly overlap and competition between programs.

If you have not already done so, you should conduct a self-examination at this point to determine why you want to develop your idea. Get rid of excessive ego involvement. The purpose of your proposal should be to help others, not to make a name for yourself. This is not to encourage false humility. From a very pragmatic standpoint, your proposal will probably be better able to stand the test of criticism if it isn't cluttered with personal, self-serving motives. If it becomes obvious that your proposal is not a good one, be prepared to drop it and help those whose ideas and programs may be more workable than yours.

Phase 3: identify potential funding sources. In the third phase of Step 2, you identify potential funding sources for your program. Although you can begin your search for funds in either the private or the public sector, we recommend that you begin with the private sector— specifically, with individual contributors. *Private individuals* contribute nearly 80% of the total amount of money given to charitable causes; this is by far the largest source available to any program. A comprehensive campaign utilizing many different methods can be developed to seek funds from individuals. Of these methods, personal, face-to-face contact is usually most effective. Share your one-page statement with any individual you think may have an interest in your program. Request a specific dollar amount to achieve the specific objective you've outlined in your proposal.

Within the private sector, you should also consider *corporations and large businesses.* This is not to suggest that such enterprises are charitable institutions; they are in business to make a profit. Basically, corporations and businesses donate funds for two reasons: to satisfy a variety of tax laws and to enhance their public image. On the other hand, corporations and large businesses are not abstract, remote, or unapproachable. They are, in fact, made up of individuals who pay taxes, hire people, lobby government, and wrestle with political realities. Study the recent funding patterns of corporations and large businesses in your community, choose three or four with whom you feel you might be successful, and make a specific request related to a specific need. Chances are good that you will receive a prompt and courteous response.

The third area of consideration within the private sector is *foundations.* There are thousands of private foundations in the United States, only about 200 of which have professional full-time staffs to handle funding requests. The Ford and Rockefeller Foundations are by far the largest of these. A complete list of foundations can be found in the *Foundation Directory,* which is available in most libraries. (See Appendix B for an annotated list of primary references to be used in researching funding sources.) Study the recent funding patterns of those institutions that might be interested in your proposal and select three or four that seem especially promising.

In the public sector, there are three levels of government that should be considered. The first of these is your local government (members of the city council and county commissioners, for example). Even if funds are not available at this level, you should secure the support of your locally elected officials. Their endorsement will expedite your requests to the state government and eventually to the federal government. The state and federal officials who review your request will attach great importance to the support it received at the local level.

STEP 3: INITIAL CONTACT

After you've researched your potential funding sources, you will be ready to implement some specific tactics in order to move your proposal to the stage of actual funding.

Draft a brief letter requesting a meeting to discuss an organization's potential interest in funding your proposal. (If a personal meeting is not practical, establish a date on which you will telephone.) Type the letter on your organization's stationery. Be sure that the letter is concise, error-free, and specific. Attach a copy of your one-page statement, and address the letter to the individual responsible for allocating funds. Follow up this communication with a phone call within two weeks. If the representatives of the funding source are willing to meet with you, it means that they are seriously considering your proposal. Once you've been able to schedule a meeting to discuss your proposal, you've successfully completed Step 3. Pause and enjoy your success while you prepare for the next step.

STEP 4: MEETING THE POTENTIAL FUNDING SOURCE

After you've received an encouraging response from a potential funding source, you should begin to develop the basic elements contained in your one-page statement by answering the following questions: Who will be hired? What is the starting date? What are the budget specifics? How does the request for this particular funding source relate to your overall funding? What is the extent of community support for your program? In answering these questions, you will be preparing an agenda for the meeting. You should try to anticipate what will happen at the meeting and anticipate the other person's response. From your point of view, the objective of the meeting is to obtain answers to several specific questions: Can you expect to receive financial support? When? How much? What special requirements are involved?

STEP 5: WRITING THE FORMAL PROPOSAL

If you can expect to receive financial support, you are ready to proceed to the last step—writing a full-scale proposal. At this point, the funding source will probably provide you with forms to be filled out or a specific proposal format that they require. Each funding source has different requirements, but all proposals contain the same basic elements: an abstract or proposal summary, an introduction, a problem statement, objectives, methods, a budget, an explanation of future financial planning, and a method of evaluation. We will now discuss each of these elements briefly.

Abstract or Proposal Summary. This will be very similar to your refined, one-page statement. Since the abstract is the first thing a potential contributor reads, it should be clear, concise, and specific. In it, you should describe who you are, explain the scope of your proposal, and estimate the cost of your program. Rarely should the abstract exceed one page, or 250 words.

Introduction. This is your opportunity to outline the strengths of your organization and its distinguished accomplishments, particularly in the field in which you are seeking support. In order to establish your credibility, you should explain how and when your organization was started, mention anything that is unique about your program, describe your organization's most significant accomplishments and goals, and list any support you have received from other organizations or from prominent individuals. (Letters of endorsement may be included in the Appendix.)

Problem Statement. Having told who you are and defined your areas of interest, you are now ready to zero in on the specific problem or problems you want to address through your proposed program. Although the primary purpose of the problem statement is documentation, you shouldn't fill this portion of the proposal with graphs, tables, and statistics: these are important, but they should be placed in the Appendix. Demonstrate the existence of the problem you want to address by referring to the sources of your evidence. Also, remember that statistics represent only one type of supporting evidence. You should also include data gathered from community groups, prospective clients, and professionals working in the field. Point out a logical connection between your organization's background and the problems you propose to address; define those problems clearly, Show that what you want to do is possible and that your goal can be accomplished within reasonable financial and time limitations. Your exercise in overcoming "white-paper shock" should be very helpful at this point.

Statement of Objectives. A program objective is a statement of a concrete, measurable result of your program within a specific length of time. For example, if the problem you intend to address is the high rate of unemployment among youth, then the objective of your program should be a measurable reduction of unemployment for this group by a certain date. Project your program into the future and carefully outline the objectives you propose to achieve.

Statement of Methods. This section deals with the specifics of how you will realize your objectives—the methods or activities you will employ to achieve the objectives you've outlined. (Refer to the ideas developed in Step 1.) In defining the activities you will conduct in order to accomplish your objectives, you should explain why you chose the particular methods you intend to use. A number of specific programs have been developed to address any given social problem. Why will your approach or methods be better than those that have already been attempted? What will be the motivation for success? What alternatives have you considered? What is the relationship between your agency and the other systems impacting the problem you have defined (the schools, the courts, the police, and so on)? What is the relationship between your agency and the community in which you will function? Who is involved in your governing body? Will you have an advisory council? At this point, the ability to conceptualize the parts of your proposal as an integrated whole becomes very critical.

Budget. Planning a budget is a specific skill that, like administration, requires considerable experience. If you need assistance in this area, you should ask other program developers for help. (They will be flattered that you asked!)

Guidelines usually call for a *line-item budget*—that is, one in which every item is reflected in a cost category. The sample budget form on pp. 22-23 will give you an idea of the general format that is followed in most line-item budgets.

Budget Narrative. The budget and the budget narrative follow the same format. The budget narrative, which can be included in the basic budget, simply provides a brief explanation of the major expenses in each item. It is particularly important in breaking down major expenses under *Miscellaneous costs.*

Future Financial Planning. This section should contain an explanation of how your organization will pay expenses that aren't included in the grant request. This enables the potential funding source to determine whether or not your organization will be able to meet its total expenses (including rent, electricity, payroll, and so on).

Evaluation. In this section of the proposal, you should answer the following questions: How do you plan to evaluate your program? What bench marks have you developed that can be measured by an independent evaluator? How do you define *success?* What will your organization be doing in five years? How does this specific proposal influence your organization's goals?

1. **Personnel**
   a.   Wages and salaries: Person in each position, job title, monthly salary or hourly-
        wage rate.

                                                Amount requested   _____

                                                Amount donated   _____

                                                Total   _____

   b.   Fringe benefits, based on a percentage of salaries and wages.

                                                Amount requested   _____

                                                Amount donated   _____

                                                Total   _____

   c.   Consultants and services, including volunteers and services done on contract, such
        as auditing and evaluation.

                                                Amount requested   _____

                                                Amount donated   _____

                                                Total   _____

2. **Nonpersonnel**
   a.   Operating area: Cost for rented or purchased space per month multiplied by the
        number of months of operation. (This includes utilities.)

                                                Amount requested   _____

                                                Amount donated   _____

                                                Total   _____

   b.   Equipment: Cost for the purchase, lease, or rental of equipment. (This includes
        office-equipment costs per month multiplied by the number of months of oper-
        ation.)

                                                Amount requested   _____

                                                Amount donated   _____

                                                Total   _____

c. Supplies: Paper clips, paper, pencils, pens, and so on.

Amount requested   _____

Amount donated   _____

Total   _____

d. Telephones: Installation, monthly charges, and long-distance calls.

Amount requested   _____

Amount donated   _____

Total   _____

e. Travel: Local travel at .15 per mile per person per month. Out of town travel for training, and so on. (Includes per diem expenses.)

Amount requested   _____

Amount donated   _____

Total   _____

f. Miscellaneous costs: All other costs are included here.

Amount requested   _____

Amount donated   _____

Total   _____

g. Indirect costs, as determined by funding source, not to exceed 10%.

Amount requested   _____

Amount donated   _____

Total   _____

SUMMARY

There are five basic steps involved in developing a program. In Step 1, you develop your idea. This often requires overcoming white-paper shock. In Step 2, you test the acceptance and feasibility of your idea and research sources of potential support. In Step 3, you implement specific tactics in order to move your proposal to the stage of actual funding. In Step 4, a personal meeting with the potential funding source usually takes place. Finally, in Step 5, you actually write a formal proposal.

Program and resource development is as much an art as a science. Although program developers should be able to use basic procedures, styles, and formats, it is the ability to conceptualize all of the parts as an integrated system that is the real key to successful program development.

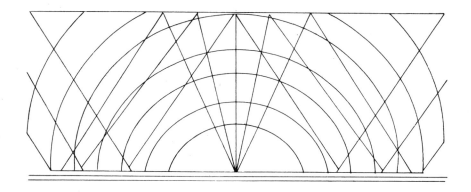

HOW TO DEVELOP GOALS AND PROCEDURES

Keith Lindblom

CHAPTER 2

"As our political and social institutions grow ever larger and more remote, the role of the small, community-based social-service agency has become that of our last, but our best, tool for building the American dream."

Keith Lindblom has been teaching for most of his adult life. His main interest is in performance-based learning, the accountability of social and political institutions, and the "repair" of broken people and tools.

We will consider the following questions in this chapter:

What are goals, objectives, and procedures?
Why are they necessary?
How are they developed?

THE IMPORTANCE OF GOALS AND OBJECTIVES

"If you don't know where you're going, you'll be somewhere else when you get there." Unfortunately, this sentence describes a dilemma faced by most institutions and many individuals. Confusion concerning goals and objectives may explain why so many people are so frequently frustrated. How many times have you worked hard to complete an assignment or project, only to be told "That's not what I wanted," "You didn't do what I asked you to do," or "Do it over again"? And you did "it" over again, never really knowing what "it" was.

The same problem arises in human-service agencies. Volunteers and staff members work long hours, often at cross purposes, in a state of frustration and tension. "Is this what I'm really supposed to be doing?" "Will my supervisor be angry?" "Will I have to do it over again?" Clearly stated and understood goals and procedures can help to eliminate frustration, confusion, and duplication of effort.

GOALS AND OBJECTIVES

A goal is a statement of a desired condition of being. Although goals are often referred to as *objectives,* the terms shouldn't be used interchangeably. You should refer to your desired end result either as a goal or as an objective and encourage every member of your staff to do the same. Consistency in this regard will eliminate confusion, especially among new staff members.

Those who take the standard school-of-business approach (management by objective, or MBO) usually make technical distinctions between goals and objectives. Objectives are thought to be narrower in scope than goals. For example, your goal might be to improve your well-being. Several objectives under that goal might be to improve your physical and mental health. Specific procedures would then be listed under each objective, indicating what you plan to do in order to achieve the objective and, ultimately, the goal. For example, a procedure under your physical-health objective might be to exercise for five minutes every morning during the next three months. This procedure describes a specific activity and defines a specific period of time in which to do it.

There is certainly nothing wrong with this distinction between goals and objectives; however, experience indicates that a great deal of confusion is created when an effort is made to distinguish between these two concepts. Throughout this chapter, then, we will use the term *goal* to refer to goals *and* objectives.

EVALUATION

In the school-of-business approach to management by objective, evaluation is used to determine the success or failure of an attempt to achieve a stated goal. Such an evaluation nearly always involves some degree of subjective assessment.

Your goal, for example, might be to improve communication between your agency and the businesses in an adjacent area. To achieve this goal, let's say that you've decided to contact a minimum of three businesses a week during the next five weeks. If you contacted that many businesses but found little or no evidence of improved communication at the end of the five-week period, then this attempt would not be considered successful according to MBO standards. Such an evaluation can have a very demoralizing personal effect on those who are involved with a project.

The standard MBO approach is to evaluate success on the basis of whether the goal was achieved. I prefer to use what I call the "Thomas Edison approach" to evaluation. After Edison had experimented unsuccessfully with over 400 elements in an attempt to develop the incandescent light, an observer remarked that he must be very discouraged because of so many failures. Edison's reply was that, on the contrary, he didn't view the experiments as failures at all, for he now knew positively of 400 elements that would *not* work.

According to the Edison approach to evaluation, it's most important *to do* the things you say you are going to do in order to achieve your stated goal. Even if you contact three businesses a week for five weeks but aren't able to improve communication, you have still succeeded in some very significant ways. First of all, you did what you said you were going to do: that should always be measured as a success. Second, you now know that the amount of effort you expended is not enough to achieve your goal. Moreover, you've accumulated very precise data—information that will be very helpful the next time someone suggests at a staff meeting that communication with area businesses could be improved if the agency would only spend a little time with one or two businesses each week.

WHY ARE GOALS AND PROCEDURES NECESSARY?

If goals and procedures are clearly defined, then communication, the unity of the staff, accountability, assessment and evaluation, and proposal and grant writing are all enhanced.

1. Communication is enhanced. Memos, reports, and verbal orders and requests can be interpreted in relationship to the goal involved. For example, if

your agency's goals and procedures are clearly understood, a request for your own telephone is less likely to be seen as an expensive "ego trip."

2. The unity of the staff is enhanced. When everyone in the agency knows how, why and when each person is to perform a particular function, individual and group roles can be clearly understood. Your work can be quite meaningful if your importance to others is clear to them and to yourself.

3. Accountability is enhanced. Requests for funds, personnel, and time can be justified with less difficulty if a clear connection between the requests and a particular goal is established. Staff members often feel more comfortable about doing their jobs when they understand clearly what is expected of them. Moreover, if a task becomes too difficult, staff members have concrete factors to examine and correct; this promotes personal and professional growth.

4. Assessment and evaluation are enhanced. When an agency's expenditure of time, money, and energy is clearly stated and related to its process and product (procedures and goals), the fundamental ingredients for assessment and evaluation are built into each program. It is more effective and fair to be judged on your own expectations than on the expectations of others.

5. Proposal and grant writing is enhanced. An agency that uses specific procedures to attain goals will accumulate a tremendous amount of data that can be used as hard evidence in requests for new or continued funding.

THE DIFFERENCE BETWEEN AGENCY GOALS AND PROJECT GOALS

Any agency has at least one long-range goal, while the projects generated by that agency will probably include short-range goals. An agency's long-range goal and its short-range project goals should never be in conflict: the long-range goal should be supported by the project goals. Each goal should be in writing and should be reviewed by staff members. Such review helps staff members to understand and support their agency's goals and keeps the agency in step with social change.

AN EXAMPLE OF AN AGENCY-GOAL STATEMENT

The following is an example of an agency-goal statement.

Subscribing to the belief that the social well-being of our community begins with the physical and emotional health of its individual residents, we have formed this agency to:

1. Formulate and state acceptable standards of physical and emotional health that should be met in the immediate neighborhood.

2. Survey our community, determine its needs, and find out which human-service agencies, if any, are presently attempting to meet these needs.
3. Plan and execute programs that will bring "what is" up to "what ought to be" in the physical and emotional health of community members.

Project-goal statements, as opposed to agency-goal statements, must clearly state "who," "what," "when," and "where." "Who" includes the doer and the receiver of "what," and "what" must include the general conditions and limits—"when" and "where."

AN EXAMPLE OF A PROJECT-GOAL STATEMENT

The following is an example of a project-goal statement.

This agency will provide regular transportation to and from nearby medical facilities for 100 neighborhood welfare recipients by June 1 of this year.

Who: Members of this agency. 100 neighborhood welfare recipients.
What: Provide regular transportation.
When: By June 1 of this year.
Where: To and from nearby medical facilities.
Why: The staff has supplied the "why" in the agency-goal statement and the community-needs assessment.

GOALS AND PROCEDURES: HOW DO THEY DIFFER?

A procedure is a statement of a process that implements the achievement of a goal. (The word *activity* may be used instead of *procedure,* but one term should be used consistently.) The same "who," "what," "when," and "where" criteria that govern the project-goal statement apply to the statement of a procedure; however, there are several major differences between goals and procedures.

Goals are general and emphasize a product or final condition; they are the ends. Procedures are specific and emphasize a process; they describe *how* a goal is to be accomplished. Procedures are the means.

If a goal is stated clearly, the procedures needed to implement that goal should be obvious. (A single goal usually produces more than one procedure.)

Assume that the project goal cited in our example arose from an assessment of the transportation needs of welfare recipients in the immediate neighborhood. The following procedures are among those that could be used to implement the goal in this case.

1. By April 10, the staff will identify and list the names, addresses, welfare status, and medical needs of 100 residents within the boundaries of (identify the target area).

2. By April 15, the staff will identify and list the names and addresses of medical facilities within a three-mile radius of the target area. (You can facilitate future references to your target area by giving it a name—Westside, Capitol Hill, and so on—after you have precisely identified its boundaries.)

3. By May 15, the agency resource director, using the medical facilities and aid recipients from previous objectives, will identify the source of funds and the amount needed to accomplish this goal.

WRITING GOAL AND PROCEDURE STATEMENTS

Goal and procedure statements are intended to inform others, not to impress them. They should be written in concise, simple, and clear language. (*The Elements of Style* [Strunk & White, 1972] is an effective aid to writing these statements.) Be precise in your use of action words, especially when you describe procedures that explain exactly what is to be done. For instance, the purpose of the first procedure in our example is to secure a list for the agency's use. Staff members might not draw up such a list if, instead of *identify and list,* the writer had used *know, really know, investigate, look into, inquire about, understand,* or any other commonly used but imprecise terms.

When expected performance levels and conditions (goals) are clearly conveyed and are *understood* by everyone involved, the assignment of resources and personnel should be readily agreed upon. When procedures are *sequential* and *relevant* to a stated goal, those responsible for assessment and evaluation are able to render maximum aid to an agency and a project. In our example, the project planner might want to rearrange the sequence of procedures by asking the staff to locate and list available medical facilities before identifying and listing those who would use such facilities.

CONFUSING GOALS WITH PROCEDURES

When writing goal and procedure statements, individuals often confuse goals with their procedures. This would be the case, for instance, if the goal statement in our example read "To raise $20,000 by June 1 of this year for the purpose of transporting welfare recipients in our community to and from nearby medical facilities." Actually, the goal is to transport the appropriate people. Raising the $20,000 by June 1 is one of many procedures that pertain to that goal. When you are writing a goal statement, always ask "why"; this will help you to distinguish between a goal and a procedure.

Goals and procedures aren't sacred. They should be reviewed often and changed whenever necessary. If the agency in our example experiences a withering of funds, the wisest move may be to alter the figure of 100 recipients. A clearly stated goal makes that remedy easy to see, however difficult it may be to carry out.

When you reach your goal or complete a procedure, you will be the first and most important person to know it. You won't have to wait for your supervisor to say "Well done!" or even "Well, done?" You will already know the feeling of success. And one success makes the next one more desirable and easier to achieve.

SUMMARY

A goal is a general statement of a condition you want your agency to effect. Generally, an objective is narrower in scope than a goal. When you refer to your agency's aim, use either the word *goal* or the word *objective* consistently. Review your agency's goals regularly. Individual project goals must be consistent with the general agency goals.

A procedure implements a goal. A goal focuses on an end; a procedure focuses on the means to that end. Goal and procedure statements must contain the *who, what, when,* and *where* of a program or agency. Goals answer the question "Why?" Procedures answer the question "How?"

A clearly stated goal enhances communication, unity of the staff, accountability, assessment, and evaluation. When a goal is clearly understood by all concerned, procedures and processes are easier to establish.

Goal statements are developed by the entire staff of an agency. Everyone must contribute ideas, understand the goal statement, agree with that statement, and review their goals in the light of each new policy decision. All goals and supporting procedures should be stated in precise action words.

SUGGESTED REFERENCES

Hall, M. *Developing skills in proposal writing* (2nd ed.). Portland, Ore.: Continuing Education Publications, 1977. This book will be valuable to you in your efforts to write grant proposals and gather data for a needs assessment. The book also includes an outstanding chapter on writing objectives.

Mager, R. F. *Preparing instructional objectives.* Belmont, Calif.: Fearon, 1962. This is a programmed book on goal specification and the step-by-step process of writing objectives that communicate to a reader. It contains sections on the significance of objectives, the qualities of meaningful objectives, and the formulation of statements of behavior and criteria.

Strunk, W., Jr., & White, E. B. *The elements of style* (2nd ed.). New York: Macmillan, 1972. A short (78 pages), highly useful reference handbook for the would-be writer. It contains sections on usage, composition, form, misused expressions, and writing style. This book is well written, terse, and to the point.

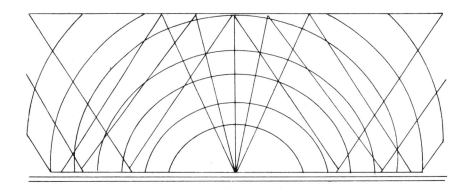

CREATIVE FUND RAISING: THE KEY TO AGENCY SURVIVAL

Don Schierling

CHAPTER 3

"Survival for small agencies frequently depends on the creative ability of the staff to raise funds for those unexpected emergencies and needs. There are so many ways to raise relatively small amounts of money that any program should view an unplanned expense at worst as normal operations and at best as an opportunity."

Don Schierling, a former community organizer and director of the Involvement Corps, maintains full-time involvement with grassroots programs. His main goal is to integrate the energies and resources of business and industry with the social goals of community-service programs.

We will consider the following questions in this chapter:

How do you identify potential donors?
What are the essential steps in planning fund-raising programs?
What should you consider when you use direct mail?
What are some of the ideas and techniques used in successful fund raising?

Most community agencies and programs have to deal with unexpected expenses that can't be anticipated even in the most carefully planned budget. A small crisis, an opportunity to take community children on a special trip, or a malfunction in a piece of office equipment may involve relatively small amounts of money, but having adequate funding in these situations can be crucial to the successful operation of an agency.

A program budget should cover the cost of essential needs for a year through major grant or funding sources, but special expenses that arise can and often *should* be met through other sources. There are several reasons for this. First, it isn't advisable to request funds from large foundations repeatedly. (The exception to this rule arises when your proposal has been rejected by a large foundation, in which case you should return with a smaller request. Foundations *do* give "conscience money," and they need the exposure that even a small award can give them.) Second, innovative fund-raising efforts give volunteers and staff members an opportunity to discover talents and energies they didn't know they had and to publicize the functions of their agency. Third, whenever you ask for money, your project is put "on the line": it must justify itself. This kind of situation provides a valuable means of self-evaluation for staff members and volunteers.

There are so many ways to raise small amounts of money that any program or agency should view an unplanned expense as an opportunity to expand its possibilities and horizons. In meeting unexpected expenses, an agency can be "liberated" from the restrictions of a static budget and the inhibitions that arise from the need to plan spending to the nth degree.

Public-opinion surveys have consistently indicated that people will contribute to social-service programs *if they are only asked* to do so; however, most agencies or programs *don't* ask, or don't ask in the right way. Confidence, born of resourcefulness, can make any program more innovative and more responsive to a variety of immediate community needs.

PLANNING AND RESEARCH

Thorough research and planning is the key to successful fund raising. You should reexamine the purpose and goals of your agency in order to determine where it has been, where it is presently, and where it is going. Having determined your agency's direction, you should be able to see how a specific fund-raising effort relates to your overall goal and then tailor the character and scope of that effort to the profile of your agency. Also, you need to take inventory of your volunteers, your clientele, and the morale and feelings of your staff.

IDENTIFYING POTENTIAL DONORS

When identifying potential donors, you need to consider every source of funds that is available to you. This is time consuming, but essential. Start with your agency's governing board, volunteers, past contributors, friends, and so on. Your agency should maintain a list of contributors; such lists are important to successful fund-raising efforts. The type of information that can be helpful to you can be placed on a 5-by-8-inch card. You should designate space on the card for the following information: name, address, phone number (work and home), zip code, place of business and type of work performed, membership in clubs, organizations and churches, previous donations (in any form), time volunteered for special projects and political activities (if relevant).

You might also want to include a check-off system on the card for such items as the number of times the donor has been contacted by your agency (and the results), whether or not the donor is a member of a sustaining fund or receives a newsletter or other form of information related to your agency. And, of course, always leave space (usually on the back of the card) for general comments and any additional information.

Contributors can be divided into three groups, based on the size of their donations. Small contributors make one *or more* contributions of $1 to $25. Medium contributors can be expected to make donations of $25 to $100. Large contributors make donations in excess of $100. Remember, it costs at least as much (and frequently more) to solicit a $10 contribution as it does a $500 gift. Small-level and medium-level contributors are most often reached through direct mail and special events, both of which require additional overhead. Consequently, the "profit" on their donations is reduced by the cost of obtaining them.

Those who contribute to your agency become personal investors, regardless of the size of their donations. As investors, they have demonstrated an interest in the success of your agency and the programs it sponsors. These people should be counted on for volunteer support and additional contributions in the future. Therefore, as you increase the number of individual donors, you increase the strength of your grassroots support and local community leadership.

FIVE STEPS IN PLANNING FUND-RAISING PROGRAMS

Almost every kind of fund-raising activity involves five specific steps. As you plan and implement such an activity, you should make sure that you've covered each step thoroughly. Insufficient attention to any of these steps will result in a loss of potential income.

Identification. First of all, you need to find out the *who, where, when, what,* and *why* of your potential contributors. *Who* is most likely to give money to your agency? *Where* can they be reached? (Are there lists available containing their addresses and telephone numbers?) *When* is the best time to ask them for their contribution? *What* is the best way to solicit them in terms of effectiveness and cost efficiency? *What* approach will they best respond to? *What* issues are they interested in? *Why* are they likely to contribute to your agency?

Message. Once you've identified and researched your potential contributors and discovered why a specific group of people would respond to an appeal, you must make sure that a message, based on your research, is delivered to as many of these people as possible.

Collection. Having decided how to reach your potential contributors, you need to carry out a collection program. When organizing the collection phase, always emphasize that the solicitor must specifically ask for money rather than hint about "needing support." Ask for a monetary contribution and, whenever possible, suggest a specific amount. One basic principle governs the various methods of solicitation—*the more personal the contact, the better the response.*

Reporting. An effective reporting system is frequently neglected as part of fund-raising programs. The reporting system should give the person in charge of the fund-raising effort an accurate indication of its progress at any given time. Moreover, the person or persons in charge of reporting should keep complete information records on all contributors.

Follow-up. Each person who contributes, regardless of the size of the gift, should be sent a "thank you" note from the agency or its governing or advisory board. Not only is this the right thing to do, but it is also critical to the positive image of your agency.

SOLICITING LARGE CONTRIBUTIONS

Reaching the potential large contributor ($100 or more) should be one of your agency's top priorities. First, try to obtain lists of the names of individuals who have given donations of $100 or more to other social-service agencies and charitable causes, or civic, consumer and public-interest groups. These names should be on public record in the Secretary of State's office. Then add the names of patrons of the theater, the arts, and special programs. These names are usually listed in brochures or pamphlets put out by the local Arts Center or individual organizations. In time, you will begin to add names given by friends of your agency who have personal knowledge of potential contributors capable of making large donations. (In these cases, note the name of the potential donor as well as the name of the friend who suggested it: they are both important to you.)

Each potential contributor will have a personal motive for making a donation. This motivation can best be determined by someone who is personally familiar with a contributor. Moreover, a personal contact is able to get your message across to a contributor effectively. Try to use someone who not only knows the prospect but also has social or business ties with the person and can deal with him or her on equal terms.

When you talk with a potential contributor, be direct about the fact that your agency needs funds and suggest a specific figure. Don't merely ask for "support" or "help." As a general rule, the amount you ask for should be more than you expect to receive. If the person doesn't wish to contribute, find out why. You may be able to clarify an erroneous impression about your agency or identify problems that should be discussed before you contact other prospects. If the person decides to make a contribution, obtain a check during the meeting or secure a signed pledge card and make arrangements to drop by and pick up the money later. *Do not ask the contributor to mail the donation.* If the donor seems concerned about making one large contribution, arrange a monthly billing or a credit-card contribution. You might also suggest contributions of stock or other items of value.

Large contributors should be asked to join your fund-raising committee and take over some soliciting assignments. If they indicate that they don't have time for this, suggest alternative forms of involvement. This is not done to exploit these people or to "get all you can." They have made an investment, and every effort should made to make them feel as though they are part of the agency.

SOLICITING MEDIUM CONTRIBUTIONS

Those who fall in the middle level—$25 to $100— are probably the most neglected of all contributors to social-service programs. Members of the $25-to-$100 group are individuals who have contributed that amount to social-service fund-raising efforts or charity drives, belong to special interest groups that might be affected by your agency, or maintain an income or social status that indicates they could contribute up to $100 if they were asked.

In compiling lists for this group, begin with the Yellow Pages listings of professions such as lawyers and doctors, whose members have the financial ability to make a medium contribution. Completing your lists will be time consuming but very worthwhile.

Direct mail, by itself or in conjunction with phone or in-person follow-up, will probably be the mainstay of your efforts to solicit small and medium contributions. When you assemble a mailing, take into consideration the number of pieces to be mailed and the number of assistants you will have. (Usually, one person can address 30 envelopes in an hour or stuff 100; therefore, a mailing of 500 pieces will require approximately 22 hours of work.)

When you use direct mail, your "package" should include the following items:

1. A letter from the president or chairperson of your board asking for a contribution.
2. A response device. This may be a card or self-mailer on which the recipient is asked to indicate the amount of the contribution and provide some personal information (name, address, occupation, and place of business). Also, there should be a space on the response device where the contributor can indicate a willingness to do volunteer work. Response devices that suggest the size of the contribution— "Here is my donation of ___$25 ___$50 ___Other"–get the best results. (If a business-reply permit is on the envelope, it will be easier for the contributor to return it to you.)
3. A brochure or fact sheet. Although this can be one of the regular pieces of information concerning your agency, it is best to include something that is aimed at the special interests of the recipient.

Direct-mail solicitation has been very successful when properly executed. Remember, writing an effective letter is only a part of direct-mail solicitation. Who is going to be on your mailing list? When are you going to do the mailing? What are you going to say?

The success of a direct-mail effort depends on a good list as well as a good letter. The best letter in the world will raise no money if it's mailed to the wrong people. The best list for your agency is one that you've compiled especially *for* your agency.

Keep the following thoughts in mind if you plan to use direct-mail solicitation for funds:

1. The mailing package consists of the mailing envelope, the letter, any enclosures, and the return envelope.
2. Test for results. Mail a random sample and evaluate its success.
3. Scrupulously edit the letter for content, accuracy, structure, readability, and appearance.
4. You shouldn't expect more than a 1% response. (However, remember that a 1% response from a mailing list of 300 will bring in $75 with an average of $25 per response.)
5. Don't hesitate to use the list more than once, especially if it is effective. In fact, in drives to raise funds from medium contributors, there should always be at least one direct-mail follow-up requesting additional funds.

You can base an estimate of how well your direct-mail program will do on the number of positive responses you received within ten days of the mailing. At that point, you should be approximately at the half-way mark in terms of responses. In other words, if you receive 20 positive replies within ten days, you can expect to receive an additional 20 within the next two or three weeks.

SOLICITING SMALL CONTRIBUTIONS

The key to successful small-gift solicitation is volume and frequency. As often as possible, you need to ask as many people as possible to donate $5 or $10. To do this, you will need programs that involve many volunteer workers, attract a large number of people, and use the mass media (public-service announcements on radio and television).

Since solicitation of small contributions is aimed at large groups or the general public, it is usually impractical to build files of individual prospective contributors. You can determine certain broad categories of potential small contributors by examining the geographic, demographic, or ethnic distinctions of groups that might have an interest in your agency or the special projects it sponsors. (Small contributors, by the way, do not necessarily have small incomes. Many people who could afford to make large contributions may not be sufficiently interested in your program or special effort to make more than a small contribution.)

The use of volunteers is particularly important in the solicitation of small contributions. With the exception of miniproposals, most of the ideas and techniques presented in this chapter require the use of volunteers.

IDEAS AND TECHNIQUES FOR LIMITED FUND RAISING

The following fund-raising ideas and techniques are designed merely to point you in some directions. As we stated earlier, planning and preparation are the keys to a successful fund-raising campaign. In this section, we will discuss the mechanics of miniproposals, sales and exchanges, lunches, walk-throughs, open houses, newsletters, special events, and other forms of limited fund raising.

MINIPROPOSALS

A miniproposal contains basically the same information that is included in a major grant request (see Chapter 1). A miniproposal should include a brief history of your agency, the names of significant groups or individuals who have participated or contributed in some way to your program, and the goals of your agency and some specific examples of its accomplishments (number of lunches served, for example). Although you shouldn't overwhelm the reader with detail, there should be adequate documentation of the successes your program has a-chieved. Detail the purpose for the miniproposal, and explain why it wasn't includ-ed in your normal operating budget. (A clear and specific budget should be includ-ed.) Large "miscellaneous" categories are not acceptable in a miniproposal. For example, a request for $1000 to finance a camping trip for underprivileged children should show cost per child broken down into transportation, meals, and so on.

If a relationship with a potential donor is well established, it may not be necessary to write such a thorough proposal. A relationship based on trust can take the place of many statistics and details, especially if the amount requested isn't large. However, your request should be clear, concise, and well written in any case. Don't abuse a good relationship with a "muddy" proposal.

You should try to establish a personal relationship with a member of an organization before you formally submit your miniproposal. People, churches, corporations, and foundations don't usually donate "cold." The personal ap-proach is always the most effective and also the most challenging. Again, prepa-ration is very important.

SALES AND EXCHANGES

Your agency can consider holding a sale or applying for the proceeds or a portion of the proceeds of a sale from another organization.

Garage sales can be fairly spontaneous, since extensive preparation usually isn't required. Specific low-cost needs can be met by the proceeds of one garage sale. For example, if someone in your organization is to attend a conference that costs $150, this amount could be raised in a short period of time. (The fact that donations are tax deductible should be emphasized when you conduct *any* fund-raising activity.)

If you need small funds regularly, you might sponsor a book exchange on certain days each month, build up a good library of donated books, and then charge a specific amount for the exchange of one book for another. The books could be borrowed indefinitely on this basis.

If your agency is on good terms with a large corporation, you might re-quest permission to have a bake sale on the premises during business hours. This would provide an opportunity for corporate employees to become better acquainted with the scope and purpose of your agency.

When you advertise a sale, it's important to tell people where the proceeds from the sale are going. People might not be interested in buying whatever is being sold, but they might buy for the cause that is being supported. *The greater the variety of reasons to buy, the better your sales will be.*

PRESENTATIONS

Many groups need speakers who can tell them about particular social-service projects—the Elks, Optimists, Jaycees, youth groups, church groups, and so on. Try to convince a particular group to sponsor or cosponsor your fund-raising campaign. If you speak at a church service, organize a special collection for your project. People enjoy giving spontaneously to a specific cause that may be more inspiring to them than the church budget. Don't be timid about passing the hat!

When you conduct a presentation, tell your audience about your neighborhood and its needs, your agency's response to those needs, your particular request, and why they should donate. The audience's response to your program will be based on how exciting the presentation is, so do your best. Slide/tape shows can be very effective when they are done properly. When you conduct a presentation, remember to make your request specific and relatively small: several hundred dollars at the most.

LUNCHES

Your agency could raise funds by sponsoring ethnic lunches for the public at regularly scheduled times. Although such lunches require considerable planning and some special resources—publicity, a food-serving facility, and "front" money for the purchase of food—once this type of event has been developed, it will sustain itself on a year-round basis. For example, a Chicano-based organization in Denver offers a Mexican meal every Friday for $2 per plate. Through this program, the organization raises several hundred dollars each year for special projects. A variety of people from all walks of life take advantage of the program. Some people come to the weekly event to see old friends, while others are interested in the projects the program supports; but all of them want to eat, and the meals are becoming an institution in the neighborhood.

WALK-THROUGHS AND OPEN HOUSES

Walk-throughs and open houses are still other methods of raising funds. Invite the public to walk through your facilities and see your programs at work, or plan a well publicized open house. You should invite the community: this includes businessmen, politicians, neighbors, homemakers, church figures, and so on. These activities represent basic public relations as well as an opportunity to obtain needed funds. As you acquaint visitors with your agency, point out problem areas and offer potential solutions to those problems. If possible, make a donation booklet available that identifies your agency's specific needs, the elements that will contribute to your program's effectiveness, and the cost of the program. With such a booklet, you can impress potential donors with your preparedness. Moreover, contributors feel satisfied when they are able to meet a small but "complete" need. You can expect to obtain more than outright contributions as a result of your walk-through or open house. Your guests might introduce you to other potential contributors, offer you assistance, or testify in your behalf to a church council or corporation board.

NEWSLETTERS

A well developed newsletter can serve a multitude of purposes (see Chapter 7). It should inform people of your agency's plans and needs. In each issue, you should highlight one specific need. (Don't swamp your audience with a multitude of requests.)

SPECIAL EVENTS

By sponsoring a big party, your agency can meet a number of goals. Throwing a party is a way of "stroking" volunteers who have helped you, providing entertainment, and raising money. Although fund raising is the underlying purpose of such a party, the emphasis of the evening should be on providing a good time for everyone.

Don't hesitate to spend a little extra money in order to make the affair a success: the "fallout" from a good experience could ensure future contributions. Take advantage of special days. Since most people go out on New Year's Eve anyway, why not offer them a party sponsored by your agency?

"Las Vegas Night" events require a great deal of organization and planning but almost always bring in money. Agencies often earn $3000 to $5000 after expenses by sponsoring such events. To sponsor one for your agency, you'll need "front money" to rent a large hall or ballroom and to provide some guarantee to the liquor distributor. Check with local "rent-all" outlets to find out where you can obtain Las Vegas-type gambling equipment—blackjack tables, roulette wheels, and so on. Local personalities can usually be drafted as volunteers to run the games, and local corporations, businesses, and political groups can usually be persuaded to donate raffle prizes.

Las Vegas Night events are legal in virtually every community; nevertheless, it's a good idea to check with the local authorities concerning procedures. While you're at it, why not ask the chief of police, the mayor, or the district attorney to volunteer an hour to run one of the tables?

Your agency could sponsor a bingo game to raise funds. You can make this game as elaborate or as simple as you like, but remember that greater preparation produces more revenue. Bingo has survived over the years because, as a fund raiser, it works.

If your agency can't sponsor a party, consider an evening out. In many communities there are country playhouses as well as restaurants that offer a play along with dinner. An agency can sometimes buy the house at a reduced rate and then sell the tickets at a higher price. Sporting events offer the same possibility of reduced rates to special groups. All of these activities capitalize on the fact that individuals are willing to "give" money for entertainment, recreation, and a good cause.

SELLING YOUR TALENTS

Your agency's clientele and staff may have skills that they would be will-int to use in order to raise funds for your program. Those who are interested in crafts could donate items, or a percentage of their sale price, to a bazaar. Such a project can help instill confidence, skills, and self-sufficiency in people who may never have been encouraged to publicly display their abilities. For example, in Applachia, a group of women from one poor community have become well known for the patchwork quilts they make, one of which was commissioned by the Rockefeller family.

MOVIES

If you have access to a meeting hall, your agency can rent movies from the local library or a movie catalog and show them weekly for cost plus 15¢ or 25¢ per person. Popcorn could be made and sold by volunteers. You'll be amazed at how quickly the nickels and dimes add up to a significant amount of money. Like ethnic lunches, this activity can be established on a year-round basis. Your movies could become the "alternative theater" in your community.

If you don't have access to a hall, you can ask a local theater owner to provide one movie showing every three months as a benefit for your program after costs are covered (guarantee this coverage to the manager). Impress upon the owner that the benefit would be tax deductible and good public relations.

LARGE IN-KIND CONTRIBUTIONS

Sometimes a tax spread can act as an incentive for a donor to give you a large in-kind contribution, such as an old automobile. Usually, contributions such as this can best be arranged with someone who has been familiar with your agency for a long time. An old vehicle can be just as valuable as cash. It could be raffled off or used as a down payment for a new van or truck or other utility vehicle needed by your agency.

DOLLAR-DAY PROGRAMS

Your agency could raise a significant amount of money in a brief period of time by organizing a dollar-day program. On a specific day, all volunteer workers are asked to collect $1 from ten or more people. You could plan to have a big party that evening and give a certificate or some other reward to those who have successfully filled their quotas.

WALKS, BIKE RIDES, AND RUNS

By organizing groups of people to take part in sponsored walks, bike rides, and runs, your agency can raise funds and provide many people with an opportunity to become directly involved with your fund-raising effort. Each participant in such an event "sells" each mile traveled to one or more sponsors for a certain price.

BYAB—BRING-YOUR-ADDRESS-BOOK DAY

Bring-your-address-book day is a variation of the Saturday-night BYOB social. Organize as many volunteers and staff members as you can for this event. Tell them to bring their address books to your agency on a particular Saturday morning. The idea here is to have each person address envelopes to the people listed in his or her address book. Although a few sample letters should be made available, you should encourage each person to develop a personal letter requesting funds. Obtain a copy of each person's letter and have it typed on an IBM selectric or similar typewriter, deleting the salutation. Locate a printer who can assure you the the ink on each letter can be matched and have 100 copies of each letter run off. There may not be 100 names ready for each letter, but people usually think of more names after the initial BYAB session. When you have the copies of the letters, ask a staff member to type in the salutation, using the names on the envelopes, and return the letters and the envelopes to the people who supplied the names. (The same typewriter that was used to type the original letter should be used to insert the salutation.) Also, you could ask those involved to donate the cost of the postage for their letters.

Although this type of effort requires a bit of organization, it is a very personal approach that can provide your agency with an immediate list of potential contributors. Most people will be able to contribute at least 30 names; therefore, if 20 show up for your BYAB day, a list of 600 names will be compiled.

SUMMARY

The key to successful fund raising, big or small, is planning and research. Build your lists and develop a comprehensive file on every potential funding source. Map your community according to demographic characteristics. Who are the people you want to approach? Where are they? Will they care about your agency or your special project if you *do* reach them?

The comprehensive planning and research techniques examined in this chapter can be used whenever your agency needs some limited funds in a hurry. If you conduct the necessary planning and research in advance, you will find it much easier to deal with your next short-term funding crisis.

Don't be intimidated by fund raising. Tap the creativity and imagination of your staff and volunteers freely, and exploit the uniqueness of your agency or project. Since there are so many methods of raising small amounts of money, an unplanned expense should be viewed as opportunity for an agency to use its resources and increase its public exposure.

Remember to thank your contributors and those who help your agency in any way. As we said earlier, expressing appreciation to these people is not only the right thing to do—the success of your future fund-raising efforts may depend on it.

SUGGESTED REFERENCES

Flanagan, J. *The grass roots fundraising book.* Chicago: The Swallow Press, Inc., 1977. To send for this basic how-to-do-it book, write: National Office, The Youth Project, 1000 Wisconsin Ave. NW, Washington, D.C. 20007.

Grubb, D. L., & Zwick, D. R. *Fundraising in the public interest.* Washington, D. C.: Public Citizen, Inc., 1976. This excellent publication covers fund-raising techniques from direct mail to door-to-door canvassing.

Knowles, H. *How to succeed in fundraising today.* Freeport, Maine: The Bond Wheelwright Co., 1976. This book covers a number of fund-raising approaches in a very comprehensive style.

Leibert, E. R., & Sheldon, B. E. *Handbook of special events for nonprofit organizations: Tested ideas for fund raising and public relations.* Washington, D. C.: Taft Products, 1972. This book includes advice on award dinners, theater benefits, fairs, house tours, and many other fund-raising methods that have been used by well established organizations. In most cases, you would have to adapt the method to fit your particular agency.

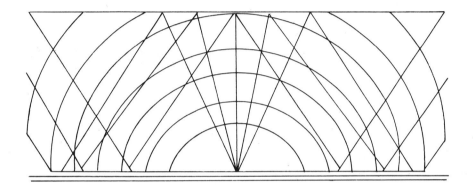

EVALUATING
SOCIAL SERVICE
PROGRAMS

Bernie Jones

CHAPTER 4

"If my hopes about the potentials of grassroot movements toward decentralization, smallness, and community self-reliance are realized, I expect to witness an exciting flowering and proliferation of varied, small community-based agencies in the areas of human service, human growth, and social change."

Bernie Jones, a consulting sociologist, is involved in program evaluation, needs assessments, design research, and community studies. In addition, he teaches at the University of Denver Graduate School of Social Work. His energies are heavily invested in the movement toward neighborhood government.

We will consider the following questions in this chapter:

What is evaluation?
Why is it necessary to evaluate programs?
Who should evaluate programs?
When and how should programs be evaluated?
How can evaluation be funded?

INTRODUCTION

Whatever the situation, the basics of program evaluation and assessment are the same. This chapter is designed to acquaint you with those basics: what program evaluation is, why it is done, who does it, and how and when it is done. As you read the material presented here, remember that you don't have to be a statistician in order to develop good evaluation techniques. It's more important to maintain a proper attitude—a belief that evaluation (accountability if you will) is the key to the ultimate success of your program. If you accept this premise, the evaluation concepts and techniques presented here will be much easier to understand and implement.

Staff members of social-service agencies need to measure how effectively they are meeting their program and project goals. This kind of evaluation has always been necessary, but with the advent of massive, federally-funded social-welfare programs in the 1960s, people began talking about evaluation as a field in and of itself.

The need for program evaluation may be recognized within an agency by administrators or a board of directors, or it may be recognized by the funding source, by disgruntled clients, or by cost-conscious legislators. The administrators of many small community-based, social-service agencies may feel that they lack the capabilities needed to perform a sophisticated program evaluation. However, evaluation has become absolutely necessary for the establishment of funding accountability, and accountability is essential to additional fund raising and, therefore, continued existence. In other words, agency administrators can no longer approach a funding source, whether it's the federal government or an individual contributor, and say "we help people." The term *help* means different things to different individuals; therefore, it's critical to the continued existence of your agency that you define your specific goals and objectives.

When goals aren't clearly identified, the entire evaluation process becomes more difficult to accomplish. The evaluator may have to work hard with agency staff, clients, and others to arrive at the best articulation of exactly what is to be evaluated. And even then, a choice may have to be made to determine which of several goals is most in need of evaluation. (That decision should *not* be made by an evaluator.)

WHAT IS EVALUATION?

Basically, program evaluation is a form of social research. In other words, the requirements that apply to research also apply to program evaluation. These requirements specify that program evaluation should be:

1. Systematic—it should be orderly and well planned, and it should follow some established procedures.
2. Controlled—that is, focused on certain phenomena or conditions.
3. Economical—research and evaluation should be cost effective to a program.
4. Empirical—that is, open to review, replication, and refutation through experience (not impressionistic or subjective).
5. Replicable—its results can be affirmed or denied through objective methods.
6. Communicable—its results can be shared easily.
7. Integrative/cumulative—it builds on what has gone before it, and it can itself be built upon.
8. Analytic—those who conduct evaluation and research should try to understand how events occur.
9. Critical—evaluation looks beyond what is and questions everything.

There are certain questions that program evaluation can answer, but there are others that it cannot answer. Evaluation can tell you whether or not a program is working. It can determine why a goal was formulated and whether or not it is realistic in light of the resources available and the environment within which a program must operate. But evaluation *cannot* answer the following questions: Is the goal worthwhile? Should the program have been funded in the beginning? Should the program be refunded? These questions concern values, and they can be answered only through a decision-making process in which differing values are debated and discussed. At times, those who evaluate programs *do* attempt to answer these questions. In doing so, however, they move from an objective to a subjective level of evaluation. It's appropriate for an evaluator to tell a board that its program isn't working or that it may never work, but it's quite another thing to suggest that a program should be terminated. An evaluator may suggest a series of alternative corrective actions to the board, but he or she shouldn't try to make a decision for the board.

Program evaluation should not try to determine who is and who isn't doing a good job. Those who evaluate programs aren't concerned with the actions of particular individuals; rather, they are concerned with the interactions that take place among particular individuals—the processes that determine whether or not a program will work.

WHY EVALUATE PROGRAMS?

The question of program evaluation isn't as simple as it may seem. One is tempted to say that programs are evaluated in order to find out how well they're working, but that's not the full story. Evaluation requires an understanding of the political context of a program and an appreciation of the values of its staff and any interested parties (such as funding agencies, clients, legislators, and so on) who have some influence on the program.

There are three general approaches to program evaluation. The first approach—often referred to as the *watchdog approach*—makes it seem as though someone is constantly looking over the shoulder of the program staff in an effort to discover errors. A much less threatening method is called the *monitoring approach*. Evaluators who use this approach simply gather information: someone else is left to decide whether or not a particular program is working. Finally, there is what we call the *social-change approach*, which views evaluation as a participatory process. Information is collected and given to staff members so that they may be better able to improve or modify their programs. The social-change approach, then, is seen as an integral part of bringing about change or improvement in the setting in which a program operates.

There are a number of specific reasons for carrying out program evaluations. The following are examples of such reasons:

1. To find out how effectively a program is meeting its goals. (Is it making any difference? To whom?)
2. To obtain information that will help restructure a program or manage it more effectively. Perhaps the evaluator wants to see if a particular component should be eliminated or replaced.
3. To identify models for others to follow, or to test a theory or an approach to a problem. (What made the program work? Can any elements be used in other programs?)
4. To find out what the staff members need to know in order to direct their program effectively.
5. To find out how well the program is working from the clients' point of view, and how it could become more effective.
6. To improve public relations and fund-raising efforts. (What will help sell a program to those whose funds or endorsements are needed?)
7. To meet the requirements of a funding source. (Is the program operating well enough to justify refunding?)

This list isn't exhaustive, but it *does* demonstrate that, in order to understand why program evaluations are needed, one must understand the political context and value orientation of those involved.

THREE TYPES OF PROGRAM EVALUATION: PROCESS, OUTCOME, AND IMPACT

There are three general types of program evaluation: process, outcome, and impact. Process evaluation deals with the administrative procedures of a program. Is the administration fulfilling its promises by hiring and training additional staff members, initiating outreach programs, filing regular reports, and so on? Outcome evaluation (sometimes called *program evaluation*) is used to determine whether or not a program is reaching its goals, and if so, how effectively. The focus of this type of evaluation is on intended consequences, such as reduced unemployment or increased services. Impact evaluations focus on the changes (intended or unintended) that a program brings about. These evaluations are, therefore, more philosophical, subjective, and impressionistic than process and outcome evaluations.

As you can see, process evaluation deals with what is going on inside a program, outcome evaluation deals with a program's final output, and impact evaluation deals with a program's effects on the immediate environment. Although it may seem difficult to differentiate among these three types of evaluations, administrators must be able to determine the kind of evaluation their programs need.

WHO SHOULD EVALUATE PROGRAMS?

There are essentially three approaches to program evaluation: a program can be evaluated by a staff member, by a consultant who isn't affiliated with the program, or by a team made up of a staff member and an outside consultant. The advantages and disadvantages of each of these approaches are summarized in Table 3.

In the "team" approach, the outside consultant helps with the design of the evaluation while the staff member gathers data. After the data is collected, the consultant might also help with the data analysis and report preparation.

WHEN SHOULD PROGRAMS BE EVALUATED?

Programs should be evaluated as they occur; that is, evaluations should begin as programs begin and run concurrently with them. In this way, evaluators can keep track of the changes programs go through as those changes occur, and they can provide periodic feedback of their findings. For example, by monitoring changes and providing feedback, an evaluator could help restructure the information-keeping systems of a program in such a way that they help the staff as well as the evaluator.

TABLE 3

Three Approaches to Program Evaluation

Approach	Advantages	Disadvantages
Evaluation by a staff member	A staff member is familiar with a program. This method of evaluation is inexpensive.	A staff member usually has little expertise as an evaluator. A staff member may be too close to a program to evaluate it objectively.
Evaluation by a consultant who isn't affiliated with the program	A consultant is likely to have expertise as an evaluator. Because a consultant isn't personally involved with a program, he or she is able to evaluate objectively.	This method of evaluation is expensive. A consultant isn't very often on the scene.
Evaluation by a team made up of a staff member and an outside consultant	Evaluations are more credible and have greater impact when formulated by a staff member and an outside consultant working together.	Evaluation methods of staff members and outside consultants usually differ.

Unfortunately, evaluation is often conducted after a program is underway or has ended entirely. Clearly, this arrangement does an injustice to the evaluator, the program staff, and the people the program is designed to benefit. An evaluation conducted at such a late stage may satisfy funding-agency guidelines, but it won't effect change or improve performance.

HOW ARE PROGRAMS EVALUATED?

Program evaluation can be done either on site or from a distance. Although each of these methods of evaluation has its advantages and disadvantages, the on-site approach is almost always more effective. When evaluation is conducted from a distance, the researcher is often unable to develop a feeling for what occurs in a program. The person conducting such an evaluation is dependent on someone else's perceptions and reports and, therefore, doesn't have an opportunity to develop the staff rapport that is essential to good program evaluation.

CONDUCTING PRELIMINARY OBSERVATIONS

The procedures for program evaluation vary from case to case, but there are certain steps that are useful in any situation. (In describing the following procedures, we will assume that the evaluation is being conducted by an outside consultant.)

An evaluation begins with preliminary observations of a program and conversations with staff members. These observations and conversations help the evaluator to form a clear statement of the scope and purpose of the program in question. Before the actual assessment is begun, this statement should be shared with the staff members to determine whether or not they agree with the evaluator's assessment. These initial steps are absolutely vital. They enable an evaluator to determine who really wants an evaluation, why they want it, who will cooperate and how, and who may resist the evaluation process.

DEVELOPING A WORKING MODEL

A basic understanding of a particular program and its context, along with a critical perspective of its operations, leads to the formulation of a *model* of that program. A model is a set of interrelated descriptive terms. The purpose of developing a model is to view a program in its total perspective.

The systems model in Figure 4-1 was used in an evaluation of an adoption agency. By using this model, evaluators were able to identify inputs and outputs related to the agency. In the course of the evaluation, the staff members of the agency became comfortable with the model and its terms. The model itself became a useful language.

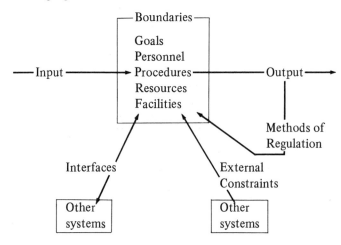

FIGURE 4-1. A systems model used in the evaluation of an adoption agency.

A working model of a program will generate a series of questions—questions that will guide the research-design and data-gathering efforts of an evaluator. Since all the questions cannot be answered in one evaluation study, the model should focus on the most important questions. For example, if your model includes an input/output scheme, then important questions will be raised regarding the origin of the input, how it makes contact with the system, what kind of outreach draws clients into the program, and so on.

DEVELOPING A RESEARCH DESIGN AND METHODS OF MEASUREMENT

After a working model of a program has been developed and significant questions have been posed, the evaluator turns to the task of developing a research design that will document the role of the program. In other words, the evaluator must devise methods of measuring changes and show that the program in question effected those changes.

The research design and the methods of measurement must be geared to the particular evaluation being conducted. (Is it a process evaluation designed to determine how well or how poorly a system is functioning? Is it an outcome evaluation designed to show whether or not a system is meeting its goals? Is it an impact evaluation that will show whether or not a system is effecting a change in its environment?) For example, if an evaluation is designed to detect changes (an outcome or impact evaluation), an evaluator needs to specify what kinds of changes are expected—changes in individuals, in agencies and organizations, or in the community as a whole. After the focus of an evaluation has been identified, a research design can be selected.

Three Types of Research Design. Basically, a research design describes the data-gathering method. There are three types of research design: experimental, quasiexperimental, and nonexperimental. Although the following descriptions of these three types are somewhat brief, we believe that a basic understanding of the key terms used in program evaluation is essential. (For a more detailed explanation of these terms, see Weiss, 1972.)

Experimental designs are most effective, because they isolate the variables, or influences, that may affect an outcome. In such a design, individuals are randomly assigned either to an experimental group, which goes through a program, or to a control group, which does not. Since individuals are assigned randomly, both groups are basically the same as they begin an experiment or a program. At the start, then, each group is measured by a variable, or factor, in which change is expected. For example, the factor in which change is expected may be body weight. If individuals are assigned either to an experimental group, which participates in a weight-reduction program, or to a control group, which does not, then a researcher may justifiably conclude that significant weight loss in the experimental group can be attributed to the program. Weight Watchers, Inc., has become famous by using this simple design. There are variations of this basic experimental design that allow even more precise identification of the sources of change (see Weiss, 1972).

Quasiexperimental designs differ from experimental designs only in that they do not feature the random assignment of individuals to experimental and control groups. Since people aren't assigned randomly, more variations, or possibilities of error, are introduced into the design—variations that weaken the reliability of the conclusions. Still, quasiexperimental designs offer the advantages derived from taking measurements at several points in time.

Nonexperimental designs offer the least amount of control of outside factors and, therefore, are the weakest form of research design. Unfortunately, this type of design is the one used most frequently in the evaluation of community-service programs. The nonexperimental design employs only one group of subjects, which is measured before and after a program is initiated.

Again, these descriptions are brief, but they should serve to make you aware of the variety of alternatives that are available in research designs. The type of design you choose will depend on the available resources as well as the conditions you face.

FOUR ESSENTIAL ELEMENTS OF EVALUATION

One way of understanding how programs are evaluated is to examine the basic elements of evaluation. These elements are: (1) the questions posed, (2) the methods used to gather data, (3) the procedures used to provide feedback of the research findings, and (4) the implementation procedures.

THE QUESTIONS POSED

The basic questions asked during program evaluation are: Is the program meeting its stated goal? (outcome evaluation), How well is the program working? (process evaluation), and What difference is the program making? (impact evaluation). At a deeper level, there may be even more analytic questions, such as: Why do that to start with? or Is a faulty program being shored up instead of challenged? or Exactly what kinds of changes are expected—changes in the people who need services, or changes in the institutions that are supposed to serve them?

Other questions that should be asked during program evaluation are: Is there any duplication of effort? Are there sufficient resources available to do the job? If not, what additional resources can be obtained? How does the program in question relate to similar programs and competing programs? How can cooperation among programs be increased? How do the board members participate in the program? Is the program open to criticism and new information? How do participants feel about themselves as a result of the program? What happens to people who aren't accepted into the program? What happens to those who aren't satisfied with the program?

A good evaluation, therefore, does more than count, weigh, and measure those who participate in a program. A critical evaluator must look for the story behind the numbers.

THE METHODS USED TO GATHER DATA

If ten people were to sit around a table on which a coffee pot had been placed, that pot would look slightly different to each of the ten people because of his or her particular position with respect to the pot. The same principle applies to a program: it looks slightly different to different individuals. In order to gain a full understanding of a program, therefore, an evaluator needs to consider a number of perspectives. Regardless of whether evaluation is conducted from within an organization or by an outside consultant, there are many ways in which staff members can and should be used in the data-gathering process. Usually, when staff members are encouraged to participate in program evaluation, modifications suggested by the results of the evaluation are easily implemented. Some of the specific ways in which staff members can participate in evaluation are described in the following list.

1. Staff members can help devise research questions. There may be particular things that bother them, or they may have questions that they would like to have resolved. For example, they may have questions such as: Why are staff meetings so unproductive? or Why can't we reach this particular segment of the population? or How can I get the rest of the staff to understand exactly what my problem is?

2. Staff members can design the research methods. They may know how to secure the cooperation and evaluative data from a particular group of people, or they may at least know what methods *won't* work with a particular group.

3. The staff can collect data. It's possible to involve staff members in some forms of data gathering, either as part of what they already do in the program or as a separate activity. (This can be arranged on either a voluntary or a paid basis.) Remember, the staff members themselves have access to much of the information an evaluator needs.

4.   Staff members can help interpret data. After raw data have been
     tabulated and analyzed, an evaluator can use the people within an
     agency to help interpret the data.

Staff participation can strengthen an evaluation. The talents and wisdom
of many people are brought to bear on the entire process. In addition, when the
research becomes their project, staff members are more likely to want to use the
results of the evaluation when they modify their program or establish new
policies.

There are three methods that can be used to gather data for a program
evaluation: (1) ask people about their behavior, (2) observe their behavior, or
(3) utilize previously collected information. An evaluator can use one method or
a combination of methods. Data can be gathered from interviews, surveys,
questionnaires, agency records, minutes from meetings, newspaper clippings, in-
stitutional records, government statistics, or ratings compiled by others.

When these methods of gathering data are carefully considered, it becomes
obvious that the researcher's "tool kit" is varied and complex and that choices
about which method, or tool, to use must be made carefully. Characteristics of
the project itself, the questions to be asked, and the population to be studied
determine which method should be used. Examples of these characteristics are
detailed in the following list.

1.   *Project Characteristics.* Available resources, such as time, money,
     energy, and skills, are some of the characteristics of an evaluation.
     Time (You can't do a mailout survey if you only have a few weeks
        to gather data. You could perhaps do a phone survey or organ-
        ize a few community meetings.)
     Money (Extended observation requires a great deal of money. In-
        formal interviews might be more economical.)
     Energy (A small evaluation team probably won't be able to inter-
        view everyone on your list in a short period of time. A mailed
        questionnaire might be best in some cases.)
     Skills (It's relatively easy to train someone to conduct a simple in-
        terview, but it's more complex and difficult to teach good
        participant-observation techniques.)
2.   *Question characteristics.* The kind of information you need will
     determine the characteristics of the questions you ask in an evalua-
     tion. Precision and sensitivity are two characteristics of evaluative
     questions.
     Precision (A few general questions could be asked over the phone, but
        the use of a series of specific questions will probably require

another approach. You might be able to obtain a general consensus of opinion at a community meeting, but not precise answers to individual questions.)

Sensitivity (People who would feel free to talk about a suicide prevention program during a face-to-face interview might be reluctant to do so in a public meeting.)

3. *Population Characteristics.* The number of people you question, and their location, life-style, level of education, and identifiability, are all population characteristics.

Number (A few dozen interviews can be conducted personally, whereas a few hundred interviews might necessitate a mail-out survey.)

Location (A concentrated population can be called together for a public meeting, but a dispersed group cannot be assembled as easily.)

Life-style (People who are accustomed to community meetings might respond well to that approach, while others might not.)

Level of Education (The level of a questionnaire must reflect the educational level of those for whom it's intended. A questionnaire that is too complicated can be both embarrassing and unreliable.)

Identifiability (Some individuals, such as former prisoners, are often difficult to identify in general society.)

Project, question, and population characteristics are the main considerations in the selection of research methods. As we have seen, the preliminary data-gathering process leads to a working model of a program, which generates specific questions. The answers to those questions suggest certain research designs and methods of measurement. The evaluator then looks at the characteristics of the project, the population involved, and the questions to be asked, and selects the appropriate research methods.

ANALYSIS AND FEEDBACK

Regardless of the method used to gather data, the data, or information, must be put into a format that is understandable and useful to the people involved in the program. There are both quantitative and qualitative forms of data analysis. Both of these forms are useful; one shouldn't be considered superior to the other.

Examples of quantitative forms of analysis are: straight tabulations (How many people were served by the program?), percentages (What percentage of people reported satisfaction with the program?), central tendencies (Which of two groups showed a higher rate of recidivism?), measures of association (What demographic factors are most closely related to success in an educational program?), and correlations (Was there a tendency for the level of satisfaction with the program to rise with the age level of the clients?).

Examples of qualitative forms of analysis are: studies (a chronological narrative of a program's history), profiles (hypothetical portrayals of program participants who underwent change), models (diagrammed presentations of events in a community program), charts (comparisons between two different groups of people), and pictures ("before" and "after" photographs of refurbished houses). Other methods of presentation can and should be developed as needs dictate. The evaluator can and should use the method that works best.

Feedback of results to those involved in a program is an essential aspect of program assessment. It shouldn't be assumed that feedback occurs only at the end of data gathering and analysis. Feedback should occur whenever it is specifically requested or whenever an evaluator has something relevant to contribute. If a program's overall goal is to provide service and effect change, then information concerning results is needed at various points in the evolution of that program. Feedback should be made available to all of those who are involved with a program. (It's often useful to prepare a brief summary of results, along with a report for those who inquire or request it.)

IMPLEMENTATION PROCEDURES

When an evaluation has been carried out properly, the information-sharing process should be relatively easy. The relationship that exists between an evaluator and those who work with the program being evaluated should allow a healthy dialogue about the report and what it might mean for the program. As we stressed earlier, decisions concerning what to do about a program's future or its funding are *not* within the purview of a program evaluator. However, an evaluator should be available to clarify information, answer questions, discuss possible alternatives, and so on. Remember, program modification is *not* the job of an evaluator.

THE COST OF PROGRAM EVALUATION

When funding for program assessment is adequate, a very professional and comprehensive evaluation is made possible. Unfortunately, circumstances often force evaluators to conduct "quickie" evaluations. For example, in a case in which a thorough evaluation might entail a large number of interviews, some direct observation, and content analysis of agency records, an evaluator might be limited to a few selected interviews and attendance at a few meetings.

If evaluation is built into a program at its beginning, expenses can be reduced by incorporating evaluation with other recurring program activities. Record-keeping forms that serve both the program staff and the evaluator could be designed, evaluative data and feedback could be shared at regular staff meetings, and questionnaires and feedback could be printed in a regular newsletter. In any case, the cost of a thorough evaluation usually represents no more than a small percentage of a program's total costs.

SUMMARY

What is evaluation? Basically, program evaluation is a form of social research. This means that the requirements that apply to research also apply to program evaluation.

Why evaluate programs? In general, programs are evaluated to maintain objective standards or to effect change. More specifically, programs are evaluated to determine how effectively goals are being met and to obtain information for future use in public-relations and fund-raising efforts.

Process, outcome, and impact evaluations. Process evaluation is concerned with a program's administrative procedures. Outcome evaluation asks whether a program is reaching its goals. Impact evaluation focuses on the changes a program effects.

Who should evaluate programs? Programs can be evaluated by member of the staff, an outside consultant, or a team made up of a staff member and a consultant.

When, where and how are programs evaluated? Programs should be evaluated on site as they develop. One way of determining how programs are evaluated is to examine the questions being asked in the evaluation, the methods used in gathering data, the processes used for providing feedback of the research findings, and the implementation procedure.

The cost of program evaluation. Evaluation costs can be incorporated into other recurring program activities. The cost of a thorough evaluation usually represents no more than a small percentage of a program's total costs.

SUGGESTED REFERENCES

Abt, C. C. (Ed). *The evaluation of social programs.* Beverly Hills: Sage, 1977. Includes articles on improving the quality of evaluation, utilizing evaluation research, and evaluating specific types of programs.

Community planning and development. Washington, D. C.: U. S. Government Printing Office, 1976. A "how-to" volume for local government officials.

Weiss, C. H. *Evaluation research: Methods of assessing program effectiveness.* Englewood Cliffs, N. J.: Prentice-Hall, Inc., 1972. One of the best introductions to the field. Contains a particularly good chapter on research design.

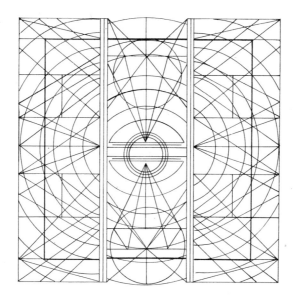

COMMUNICATIONS
PART TWO

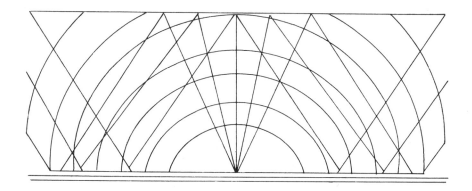

WRITING AS A COMMUNICATION TOOL

Marie Alexander

CHAPTER 5

"In the administration of small community-based, social-service agencies, every skill and every ounce of character you possess is needed in order to engage in real helping relationships and, at the same time, to keep the program functioning. These agencies, however, are the only viable alternatives to huge, faceless, federal and state bureaucracies. Through sound management skills and a genuine concern for people, these programs are meeting the real needs of the neighborhoods and communities they serve."

Marie Alexander maintains an active involvement in all areas of program development and community-service administration. She has helped develop a drug-rehabilitation program, a program for senior citizens, and a training program for staff members and administrators of residential facilities for the developmentally disabled. She is currently the director of Federal-Program Development at Metropolitan State College in Denver.

We will consider the following questions in this chapter:

What are the basic forms of written communication used by social-service agencies?
How can you decide which form to use?
What are the steps to writing an effective report?
How can you tell if your report will be effective?

INTRODUCTION

When we think of communication, most of us think of speech. We tend to feel comfortable when we talk to one another. Feedback is immediate. We can revise and clarify our message as we deliver it. Our body language, facial expressions, tone of voice, and tempo all add dimension to our words and reinforce the message they convey. When we write, on the other hand, we are solely dependent on symbols that we string together in an effort to deliver complex emotional and intellectual messages. We receive no feedback until we've already made decisions and committed ourselves to a particular verbal structure. The burden of responsibility and clarity is on us.

The same fixed characteristics of writing that sometimes make us reluctant to commit ourselves to paper also make writing a powerful business tool. Because the written word is fixed and visual, you can convey a piece of information to many people over a period of time through written communication. You can permanently document activities, secure firm agreements, express complex business needs and relationships, and organize and communicate tremendous quantities of information. Those who read the information can take time to assimilate the ideas and facts you present and attempt to understand the thought processes that led you to your conclusions. Written reports can also be a strong, unifying force that knits together the efforts of staff members and volunteers.

The practical challenge to administrators and staff members of social-service agencies is to recognize the usefulness of written messages within the activities of their jobs and realize that they already possess the skill they need to write effectively. Almost every agency position requires the ability to analyze, think clearly, make decisions, and influence others. In writing reports, an individual simply applies these skills.

This chapter provides an overview of the forms of written communication used by social-service agencies and attempts to establish useful guidelines and suggestions to help you choose the right form at the right time and use written communication as an effective tool.

CHOOSING THE BEST FORM OF WRITTEN COMMUNICATION

Since social-service agencies convey information on a variety of subjects dealing with every phase of their operations, many forms of written communication (reports) come into play. However, every report is a factual presentation of information directed toward a specific audience for a definite purpose. The form, content, and organization of the report are means to an end. The ultimate aim is always effective communication.

In order to decide which type of written communication would be most effective in a particular situation, ask yourself the following questions:

What is my purpose?
What objectives do I intend to accomplish?
How complicated is my subject and what kind of treatment does it require?
Do I need graphs, charts, and tables?
How long should the report be in order to cover the material adequately?
What are some of the interests of my intended audience?
How much time should I spend preparing this report?
How much time can I afford to spend?
What is the value of the report?
Will I be addressing a topic of real importance or am I dealing with a subject of temporary significance?
What characterizes my relationship with the intended audience?
Is formality appropriate?
How do I intend to use the report?
How will the report be distributed?

If your answers to these questions suggest that you are dealing with subjects or problems of current or temporary interest in an informal situation, you should prepare to write an informal report. The following section describes some frequently used informal reports. Formal reports, which deal with subjects of relative significance, will be treated in another section.

INFORMAL REPORTS

As an administrator of a social-service agency, you will probably use short, informal reports quite often. These are the written messages people use as tools to conduct their day-to-day business. As their name implies, informal reports are written for informal situations dealing with current topics. They usually vary in length from one to ten pages. There is usually no need for a title page or a cover. The pages of informal reports are most often paper-clipped or stapled together.

The most frequently used informal reports are: memoranda, letter reports, bulletins, booklets, minutes, and short reports. We will now discuss each of these in detail.

MEMORANDA

Memoranda, or memos, are most often used for internal communication, although they can be sent to individuals outside an agency if the format is appropriate to the situation. A salutation isn't included in a memorandum. Space is provided for the name of the person who writes the memo, the name of the individual to whom it is addressed, a brief description of the subject matter, and the date. The person who writes the memo signs or initials it at the end of the message. This format is designed for clarity, quick reading, and easy retrieval after filing.

The message in a memo is written in a straightforward, impersonal manner. Unlike a letter, which might be used to introduce a subject or persuade a reader to a particular action, a memo is used to speed the flow of information. You might use a memo to call or cancel a meeting, ask for figures used in compiling statistics, or communicate information that is needed to coordinate programs. A memo could also be used to clarify or document informal working agreements. At times, memos are used to route long, formal reports through specific channels.

The following example illustrates the format we've discussed here.

To: Supervisors—Alice Rubiano, Betty Smith, and Jim Williams
From: Carol Perkins, Accountant
Subject: Travel reports for volunteers

Beginning next pay period, travel reports for the volunteers working with your staff must be approved by you.

Please check all reports to be sure the mileage is appropriate. Then sign the reports and have them delivered to the bookkeeping department. Some of your volunteers seem to have difficulty copying odometer readings. For example, 42.5 miles sometimes appears as 425 miles or 4.25 miles. These and other mathematical errors can (and should) be corrected by the supervisors who schedule the volunteers.

The first paragraph in this example describes the decision to be implemented. The second paragraph makes particular requests and offers reasons for those requests. Each step, or component, of a message in a memo should be separated for clarity. The format used may vary a great deal, but the message must be clear and to the point.

Little investigation is needed for most of the memoranda you will write. However, when memos are used to present analyses and recommendations in addition to information, each step should be developed in a separate paragraph with its own subject heading.

LETTER REPORTS

Letter reports are letters that contain information or deal with problems. They are similar to business letters in layout, but not in style. Letter reports are less personal than business letters, and they focus on a direct, factual presentation. Although the material in a letter report is tightly organized to conserve the reader's time and effort, it communicates all the information that is needed.

Tables, charts, and graphs that support or clarify your conclusions should be enclosed with a letter report. Although such material might help to substantiate your interpretation of the facts, its inclusion in the body of the letter would interfere with the readability of the report.

The following example of a letter report illustrates the format and style we've discussed here.

Name and address of your agency

Date

Name and inside address

_____

_____

_____

Subject, or reference, line

Salutation

(Introduction) A statement of the problem and the reason for the report. This paragraph familiarizes the reader with the problems the report addresses.

(Summary) A summary of your findings, conclusions, and recommendations.

(Development of the report) Explain how you reached your conclusions and recommendations. Describe the methods you used to collect data and facts.

(Concluding Statements) This includes suggestions, proposals, recommendations, requests, or specific actions to be taken.

Complimentary closing
Your signature
Your name (typed)
Position

Your initials
A list of enclosures

BULLETINS

Bulletins are used to communicate information to agency members or to individuals outside an agency. Each bulletin deals with a single subject and is directed to a large audience. Bulletins vary in length from one to three pages. They can be posted on walls or fastened together as small booklets. They may or may not be labeled as bulletins. If a bulletin is long, paragraphs may be numbered for easy reference. Clarity and readability are the most important criteria to keep in mind when you are preparing a bulletin.

You might use bulletins to announce personnel changes, agency policies, service procedures, funding changes, or regulations that influence hiring practices. Bulletins also might contain suggestions for improving skills or job performance.

BOOKLETS

Booklets are very similar to bulletins. They are informative, and they are used for internal as well as external communication. However, booklets deal with subjects of long-range interest and importance. The style and general form of a booklet is determined by its purpose and its intended audience. In any case, a booklet should be attractive and inviting.

You might want to develop a booklet to give volunteers an overview of their role within your agency. In a booklet, you could explain your agency's background, philosophy, and goals to prospective board members. New employees might benefit by having a booklet that outlines your agency's policies, procedures, and benefits. Recipients of services might need the information contained in a booklet that describes your agency, its role in the community, and the programs it offers.

MINUTES

Minutes must be accurate, clear, and complete. They represent the legal documentation of policy for an agency. In the minutes, credit must be given to individuals who present reports and introduce motions. The most important items listed in the minutes are the responsibilities that are delegated and accepted within an agency.

An individual who records minutes places the time and place of the meeting at the top of the page. Next, the names of those who are present and members who are absent are listed. The business of the meeting is noted as it takes place. Paragraphs may be numbered to identify points discussed and actions taken.

Rearrangement of the material in the minutes under subject headings requires time to decide what is important and how it should be emphasized. Nevertheless, when material is organized according to subject matter, minutes become more interesting, and readers can easily find the information they need to make decisions and develop reports.

The usefulness of minutes is illustrated by the practices of an organization called *The Downtown Consortium*—a group of people representing agencies that deliver services to elderly people in the downtown area of a large city. This group meets once a month to discuss mutual problems, joint program planning, and case management. Minutes of the meetings are mailed to members of the agencies represented to keep them informed, serve as a reminder of commitments they've made, and provide contact that contributes to group vitality and cohesiveness.

The following example illustrates the points we've discussed here concerning the style and format of minutes.

RESIDENTIAL SERVICES   COMMITTEE MINUTES
Residential Services Office
October 27, 1979

The meeting was called to order at 1:40 P.M. Those Present were:
Kay Grant—Parent, Chairperson
Fred Hopkins—Synthesis
Jane Givens—Parent (Guest)
Margie Stearns—D.A.R.C. Residential Committee
Roger Buchanan—Protective Services
Absent were:
Clara Carson—Ministry for the Handicapped
Georgia Clinton—Autism Society
There were no corrections to the minutes of the last meeting.

Workshops. The idea of a training workshop was introduced. The consensus was that this is not the right time—that the idea should be held in abeyance until there is a need for a concentrated work session after goals and objectives have been identified.

Report on the State's Residential-Services Meeting. Clara Carson was to make a report on the State's Residential-Services Meeting with Rudy Durkin, of the Division for Developmental Disabilities, and the state-wide residential providers. This was tabled until the next meeting.

Transfer of Planning Grant. Kay Grant informed the members of this committee that the D.A.R.C. may transfer the Residential-Services Planning Grant to The Downtown Consortium Board. This would mean that the Downtown Consortium Board would assume the Grant for the duration of the year. The transfer will provide the means by which this planning committee will coordinate existing programs and develop and implement a system of new programs.

State's Continuum. Since the state's continuum is going to be revised, a recommendation was made that this committee define a service continuum to be presented to the State Task Force on Residential Services.

The committee members were asked to complete the questionnaire distributed at this meeting and the Service Provider's Questionnaire, which had been mailed to them.

The meeting adjourned at 4:15 P.M.

SHORT REPORTS

Informal short reports, which vary in length from one to three pages, contain a title page, an introduction, a summary, a discussion section, and a supplementary section.

Title Page. The title should give a clear, concise statement of the scope of your project. The title page should identify the report by subject, agency, author, and the date the report is submitted.

Introduction. The Introduction should give the reader appropriate background information. It lets the reader know what the report is about, by answering questions such as: What are the objectives of your project? Why is this situation being investigated? Why should the reader be interested? How does this situation relate to other agency activities? In the introduction, you create a perspective through which the reader can relate to your goals.

Summary. Your conclusion should be based on sound logic and a realistic interpretation of the facts. It should be brief and to the point. If you're unable to draw a specific conclusion, you should summarize the main points or results of your investigation. In some instances, conclusions and recommendations might *follow* a summary of your report.

Discussion Section. This section contains the details that led to your conclusions and recommendations. In the discussion section, you support and explain each decision and issue in your report. You might want to begin by amplifying some of the subjects mentioned in the Introduction. For example, you could explain how you conducted your investigation, how you chose your research design, and what you observed during the research process.

Graphs, charts, and tables should appear where they function best. Those that are significant should be included in this section. Less crucial information belongs in a special section at the back of the report, or in the Appendix.

Supplementary Section. Material that relates to the subject but is not an integral part of the text belongs in a supplementary section. Complete tables from which smaller ones have been taken, charts that are too cumbersome to place in the text, references, lists of symbols and terms, sample questionnaires, interview forms, and reporting forms are examples of such material.

STEPS TO WRITING AN EFFECTIVE REPORT

Since writing, as McLuhan says, "is the wondrous art of painting SPEECH . . . to embody, and to colour THOUGHT" (1967), then words are the medium, and, as such, they are the tools of organized thought. To use words effectively, you need to organize the thoughts you intend to "embody." In order to write an effective report, you need to plan your strategy, analyze the situation your report deals with, take notes, define the scope of your report, develop a working plan, and organize your information.

PLAN YOUR STRATEGY

When you plan your strategy, you decide to follow certain procedures. What are you going to do? How are you going to do it?

ANALYZE THE SITUATION

What is the purpose of this report? Earlier in this chapter, you asked yourself this question to help you choose the most appropriate form of written communication. The question bears repeating until you have a perfectly clear idea of *why* you are writing your report, *what* you intend to accomplish, and *who* will read the report. In answering these questions, you begin to analyze the problem or situation your report addresses. This analysis, or examination of the elements of a situation, should help you to define the problem you intend to address.

TAKE NOTES

As you clarify your goals and objectives, you should begin to take notes of relevant facts. These notes will help you develop a guide for your investigation. Moreover, they could be rewritten as an outline for your report.

When you take notes and formulate an outline, you should consider questions such as: What kind of information would best accomplish my goals? What are the main issues and problems involved? What are some of the possible solutions? How can my information be best organized to persuade the reader?

You should identify the main elements of your report in subdivisions. The following examples represent a few of the many patterns a general outline might assume:

Example A
    Problem
    Causes
    Results
    Possible solution
    Discussion
    Pros and cons
    Recommendations

Example B
    Conclusion
    Evidence
    Alternatives
    Discussion
    Summary

Example C
Summary—what has been done
Work to be done
Future plans

DEFINE THE SCOPE OF THE REPORT

You can't say *everything* about anything. Decide on the extent of the material you can reasonably expect to cover in the time and space allowed. Focus on the material as though you were taking a photograph. Through the lens of a camera, you limit the subject and establish a perspective. Based on the information you've gathered, you can focus on your specific purpose, limit your subject, and begin to arrange your message.

DEVELOP A WORKING PLAN

By now you should have a clear idea of what you want to do. Your working plan explains *how* you are going to accomplish your goals. Occasionally, a proposed working plan for an investigation and report must be written and submitted for approval before a project is initiated. When this is the case, the working plan can take the form of either a letter or an outline. The amount of detail you include in a working plan is determined by skills, the limitations of time and space, the intended audience, and the purpose of the report. A working plan may include any or all of the following elements:

1. A clear statement of the problem you intend to address.
2. The ways in which the report can be used.
3. Your goals and objectives.
4. A breakdown of the components of the problem you intend to address.
5. The limitations of your report.
6. The procedures used for gathering data (research design, interviews, questionnaires, observations, and so on).
7. Your sources of information.
8. The methods you used to organize your information.
9. A tentative outline.
10. Tentative conclusions.
11. An estimate of the amount of time and money needed to implement your recommendations.
12. A work schedule.

ORGANIZE YOUR INFORMATION

Pull Your Information Together. The first step you need to take in organizing the facts and ideas you've collected is comparable to separating apples from oranges. You need to organize your information according to categories before you can use it. There are four basic kinds of data, or information: (1) quantitative data (such as numbers, amounts, or the results of a questionnaire), (2) qualitative data (such as ideas and facts, or the notes you've accumulated through interviews and research), (3) chronological data (such as the changes observed in a program over a period of time), and (4) geographic data (such as the characteristics that influence plans for a regional delivery system).

PREPARE A DETAILED OUTLINE

Most reports are made up of three main parts: an introduction, a presentation and analysis of information (the body), and conclusions and recommendations. There are no inflexible rules concerning the construction of your report. For example, you might open your report with a statement of the problem, or you might begin with your recommendations. Although everyone expects a beginning, a middle, and an end in everything, the organization of agency reports can vary greatly.

Once your material is fairly organized and you have some sense of the logical flow of thought through your report, you are ready to work on a detailed outline. If you have been jotting notes or drawing up tentative outlines throughout the planning process, you should now clarify relationships and check to be sure that your divisions and subdivisions are parallel in construction.

An outline divides a report into its major components and shows how each part is related to the others. A carefully prepared outline will save you time when you begin to write your report. In addition to helping you to write a concise, direct, and purposeful report, an outline can suggest the subject headings that will appear within the report and in the table of contents. Moreover, a carefully prepared outline can serve as the basis for a summary of a report.

WRITING THE FIRST DRAFT OF YOUR REPORT

You should write the first draft of your report quickly, without concern for grammar or punctuation. The flow of thought and the development of supporting material are the most important considerations at this point. Let yourself relax into a mental dialogue with the intended audience. Think through your ideas as though you were discussing them. Look at your ideas form the reader's point of view. Anticipate responses, and react to those responses. As thoughts occur to you, allow yourself to move away from your outline. The creative space you allow between the outline and your new insights can improve your report significantly.

When you write a report, you are preparing to guide a reader through a thought process. The introduction sets up an orderly path—an overview of the terrain. In the introduction, you paint an emotional and intellectual landscape with words. It's your responsibility to point out changes, shifts, and significant points along the way; this necessitates the careful use of transitions and subject headings.

Remember to point out the ways in which your information relates to a particular problem and to the reader's interests. Tell the reader what is important and why. When you reach a conclusion, be sure that the reader has been persuaded to draw the same conclusion and accept your recommendations.

CHECKING THE EFFECTIVENESS OF YOUR REPORT

The easiest way in which you can judge the effectiveness of a report is to evaluate its end results. (Did the agency change its policies? Were the services you suggested implemented? Did the board decide to purchase the equipment needed to expand the program?) However, you also need to measure the effectiveness of your report before it is presented. The following questions can be used as a checklist in this regard:

1. Does your report change the situation that prompted it? Do your recommendations fulfill the purpose of the report? Does the report address the reader's needs?
2. Is your report carefully organized? Is the planning thorough? Are the main issues sufficiently emphasized?
3. Are the facts in your report accurate? Are quotations, charts, and tables accurate? Is the information complete?
4. Is the form of your report appropriate to its purpose, its intended audience, and its message?
5. Is your writing style clear, easy to read, and easy to comprehend? Is there a smooth flow of thought from one idea to another?
6. Is your report interesting?
7. Are visual aids used logically and effectively?
8. Is your conclusion adequately supported by specific evidence? Is your conclusion clearly logical?
9. Will your report motivate action?

If after you answer these questions, you decide that your report isn't effective enough, you should revise your material and rewrite your report. A report that is badly written is a waste of time for all concerned, a poor reflection on the credibility of an agency or a department within an agency, and a potentially destructive tool that could provoke inappropriate action.

REVISING AND REWRITING YOUR REPORT

Up to this point, we've emphasized the importance of including all the necessary information in your report. When you revise and rewrite it's also necessary to judge *how* your information is presented.

Check your report carefully for adequate development, clarity, accuracy, and consistency in the following areas:

1. *Mechanics*
     Spelling
     Punctuation
     Grammar
2. *Form*
     Appropriate type of report
     Margins
     Paragraphing
     Footnote form
     Bibliographical form
     Subject headings
     Consistency
3. *Organization*
     Relationship of parts
     Sequence of ideas
     Transitions
     Unity
4. *Expression*
     Specific facts and details clearly expressed
     Varied sentence structure
     Short sentences predominant
     Smooth phrasing
     Use of topic sentences
5. *Use of Words*
     Concrete
     Familiar
     Precise
     Simple
     Abstract concepts and specialized terminology defined

6. *Adaptation to the reader*
    Appropriate level of readability
    Appropriate tone
    Consideration of the reader's experience, knowledge, and interests

If you aren't familiar with the basic techniques you need in order to develop your ideas, or if punctuation makes you uncomfortable, don't hesitate to consult a reference book. Correct form is essential!

PROOFREADING YOUR REPORT

After you've completed the first draft of your report, a proofreader reads the copy as a whole and checks it for form, layout, and mechanical accuracy. The final copy should be nearly perfect, particularly if your report is to be widely distributed. The final copy also should be checked against the first draft to be sure that the typist hasn't left out any part of the report.

FORMALIZING YOUR REPORT: PRELIMINARY AND SUPPLEMENTARY SECTIONS

Now that you have a polished report, you will want to include preliminary and supplementary sections to make the report appear formal and impressive. These sections are functional as well as cosmetic. The preliminary sections present material that explains and identifies the report and the situation for which it was prepared. Supplemental sections refer to the report itself and include material of a general and secondary interest for reference purposes. Occasionally, material that is too bulky to be included in the text is placed in a supplemental section.

PRELIMINARY SECTIONS

The following items appear in the preliminary sections of a formal report: the cover, title page, table of contents, list of tables, and summary.

Cover. The title, author, and completion date appear on the cover, which protects and identifies the report.

Title Page. The title page identifies a report by providing the title, subtitle, author (including his or her position and address), the name and address of the agency or company for whom the report has been prepared, and the date of completion. An effective title is one that catches the reader's attention and tells him or her what the report contains (who, what, when, where, why, and how). The title should be accurate, concise, and descriptive. Delete all unnecessary words from the title ("A Survey of" or "A Report on," for example). The following suggestions should help you to compose effective titles:

1. Use a subject and a verb.
2. Refer to the action the report suggests.
3. Indicate the expected results.
4. Indicate the scope of the report.

An example of a formal blocked title page appears below. (The same information could be centered instead of blocked, depending on the style you prefer.)

Letter of Transmittal. The letter of transmittal forwards a report to the group or person for whom it was prepared. The letter is written after a report is completed. It can be bound with the report following the title page or attached to the cover or title page.

Improving the Cost-Effectiveness of Home Health Service

Identification of Different Service Levels to Effectively Reduce the Cost of Service per Person per Year

Prepared for:
Margaret Jackson
Executive Director
Home Health Services, Inc.
8900 Winnow Way
Salt Lake City, Utah

Prepared by:
Martin Sommers, Ph.D.
Consultant
New Skies, Inc.
700 Colfax
Santa Fe, New Mexico

June 22, 1980

Table of Contents. The table of contents is a topical outline of the material contained in a report. Generally, no more than three levels of headings are listed in the table of contents. (The longer the report, the more detailed the subdivisions.) Major headings are typed in capital letters. Subheadings are typed in upper/lower case. If you decide to list the preliminary and supplementary sections in the table of contents, you should type them in lower case.

List of Tables. A list of tables may be included if charts, tables, photographs, or figures appear in a report. You can call it a *Table of Charts,* a *Table of Illustrations,* or whatever name applies to the material you've included in your report. In a list of tables, the tables appear in the order in which they appear in the text of the report. When there are only a few illustrations or tables in a report, they can be listed at the bottom of the table of contents or as subdivisions in their appropriate place in the table of contents.

Summary. The summary can appear in the letter of transmittal, or it can be written as a separate part of the report that completes the preliminary section.

The letter of transmittal may include any or all of the following elements:

1. A reference to the authorization of the report that states the terms under which an investigation and report were to be made.
2. A summary of the report.
3. History and background.
4. Scope and limitations of the report.
5. An explanation of the need for the report.
6. The intended use of the report.
7. Conclusions and recommendations.
8. Personal attitudes and opinions of the report's author.

The importance of a good summary cannot be overstated. Some readers will read *only* the summary. Their decisions will be based on how well you represent your investigation and report. Those who read the entire report will use the summary as a reference tool.

In the summary, direct, concise writing is essential. Each section of the report should be represented in proportion to its importance. Only information that appears in the report should appear in the summary. A carefully prepared outline can be used as a base when you are preparing the summary.

SUPPLEMENTARY SECTIONS

The Appendix. This is where you include the material that would get in the reader's way if it were in the body of the report. The appendix includes, but is not limited to: letters, copies of questionnaires or evaluation forms, detailed data, a glossary, and large tables. The contents of this section can be grouped together or placed in separate appendixes (Appendix A: Questionnaire, Appendix B: Letters, and so on). The form is up to you.

The Bibliography. The bibliography may be included in the appendix or as a separate section of the report. In this section, you list all the printed sources you used in writing your report and collecting your data. The sources are listed in alphabetical order according to the last name of the author.

SUMMARY

Before you write a report, you need to ask yourself the following questions: What's the purpose of the report? What kind of treatment does the subject require? Who are the intended readers and how interested are they in the subject? How much time should you spend on preparation? Of what value is the report? How formal is your relationship with the readers? Will the information in the report be used?

The most frequently used forms of informal written communication are: memos, bulletins, letter reports, booklets, minutes, and short reports.

Memos are used most often for internal communication. They are usually straightforward and fairly impersonal. They speed the flow of information and document the fact that information has been passed along.

Bulletins are used for internal and external communication and are usually intended for a large audience.

Letter reports contain information the reader needs in order to understand a particular situation. They are less personal than conventional letters.

Booklets are longer than bulletins, but they perform similar functions.

Committee minutes must be accurate, clear, and complete. Proper credit must be given to people who give reports, make motions, and delegate and accept responsibilities.

Short reports contain a title page, an introduction, a summary, discussion sections, and any necessary supplementary sections.

In order to write an effective report, you need to plan your strategy, analyze a particular situation, take notes, define the scope of your report, develop a working plan, and organize your information. After you've organized your material, you should prepare an outline and write the first draft of your report. Ask yourself whether your first draft really meets your criteria. Revise and rewrite if necessary, and then proofread your final copy.

Preliminary and supplementary sections are added to more formal reports. Preliminary sections contain information that explains and identifies your report and the situation for which it was prepared. The cover, title page, letter of transmittal, table of contents, list of tables, and summary all appear in preliminary sections. Supplemental sections (the appendixes and bibliography) contain information that would get in the reader's way if it were presented in the body of the report.

SUGGESTED REFERENCES

Brown, L. *Effective business report writing.* New Jersey: Prentice-Hall, Inc., 1973. An exhaustive treatment of the subject with considerable attention paid to research reports. The chapters on visual aids and oral reports could be useful. The material was developed for businesses, but the principles presented can be adapted to social-service agencies.

Baker, S. *The complete stylist.* New York: Thomas Y. Crowell Co., 1972. Most of the material focuses on organizing, developing, and presenting information. Baker's is a sound, readable, useful text that thoroughly covers the principles of writing.

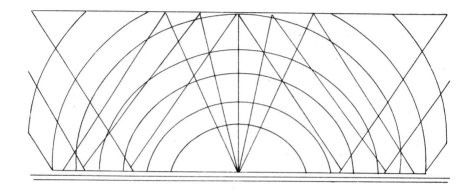

HOW TO
DEVELOP
AN AGENCY
NEWSLETTER

A. G. Eisenman

CHAPTER 6

"Small community-based, social-service agencies can and must choose their own directions and roles. No small agency can effectively plan for tomorrow if it is constantly reacting to the direction and purpose determined by someone else. Given the nature of today's bureaucratic politics, the successful small agency of the future will be the one that becomes the actor, rather than the reactor."

A. G. Eisenman has developed a step-by-step illustrated manual that describes the production of monthly newsletters. He teaches a course in practical community journalism and maintains an active interest in political philosophy and consumer-oriented movements.

We will consider the following questions in this chapter:

What is the purpose of an agency newsletter?
What materials are needed to produce a newsletter?
How are the costs of production determined?
How is a newsletter financed?
What are the major technical steps involved in producing a newsletter?
How can you build the circulation of your newsletter?
How can you evaluate your final product?

THE PURPOSE OF A NEWSLETTER

Before we discuss the processes involved in developing an agency newsletter, we would like to examine the functions of such a publication. Any newsletter can be used to raise funds, publicize news, opinions, and announcements, and create a community or agency consciousness.

In some respects, a newsletter is similar to a newspaper. It is intended for readers rather than television viewers or radio listeners. Moreover, each page of a newsletter must be laid out carefully so that the final product is visually attractive. Finally, like the newspaper editor, the producer of a newsletter must assign priorities to news and information. These priorities are determined by the interests of the audience and the limits of space.

A newsletter should serve as a mirror, reflecting the activities of an agency, the important programs and services that exist in the agency's community, the opinions of the members of the community, and the history of the agency and its community.

The following items could be included in an agency's newsletter:

1. News and announcements concerning the agency.
2. News and announcements concerning the community.
3. Specialized news and announcements (sections for senior citizens, the handicapped, and so on).
4. Opinions of agency members and community members.
5. The organizational makeup of the agency and its staff of officers.
6. This history of the agency and the community in which it operates.
7. The agency's tutorial program.
8. The agency's training program.
9. Letters from readers.
10. A profile of the agency's clientele (past and present).

MATERIALS NEEDED TO PRODUCE A NEWSLETTER

In order to produce a newsletter, you will need the following materials: a ruler, a pair of scissors, graph paper, typing paper, rubber cement, a bottle of correction fluid, a black felt-tip pen, black ink, several sheets of rub-on lettering, a typewriter, and a pen. The ruler and scissors are one-time purchases, but they are important. Buy a pair of scissors that cuts sharply and cleanly, and look for a ruler that is strong and flawless. As far as paper is concerned, you should search for quality at bargain prices. For typing, any white paper except onion skin will do. Graph paper is used for lay-out sheets, because it provides blue grid lines that a printer's camera can't photograph. These grid lines will prove helpful when you paste up materials in straight, even lines.

Sheets of rub-on lettering are expensive, but, unless your agency employs a graphic artist who is capable of drawing lettering of various sizes and styles, they are essential. You should start with at least five sheets of different styles and sizes of lettering. (There is obviously no need for lettering as small as the size of standard typewriter type.)

A typewriter is essential to the production of a newsletter. The quality of the typewriter, of course, will directly affect the quality of your newsletter. If you have a typewriter with interchangeable typeheads, the varying type styles can increase the attractiveness of your newsletter. In addition, different type faces can be used for headlines, news copy, titles, italicized items, advertisements, announcements, and photograph captions.

When you've obtained these materials, you will be ready to produce your newsletter.

PRODUCING A NEWSLETTER

You can't produce a newsletter before you've gathered the raw material—the information—that is to become the most important part of that publication. Collecting information is a critical part of the total production of any newsletter. You should read at least one newspaper every day to look for the following items: stories that concern the scope of your agency's work, publicity that is focused on programs related to your agency's realm of concern, news and features of interest to the community in which your agency operates, and news features about events or people in that community. This step represents an important beginning. Your research will provide information for your newsletter while you gain invaluable experience in searching for information and material that is relevant to your readers. You may "borrow" items from the newspaper (as long as you acknowledge your source)—you cannot assume that your readers have already seen the material you've researched.

You should also gather information and news from within your agency. This includes items regarding announcements, activities, personalities, meetings, and any agency requests for community input. If there is an abundance of this kind of material, your greatest difficulty will be in selecting the most important items and writing as concisely as possible. You shouldn't have to painstakingly search out such information from within your agency: news and information that has to be drummed up cannot be worth much. If your agency has nothing to publicize, don't try to create news. The simple fact is that your readers will know whether or not you are trying to portray your agency honestly.

Your third source of news and information is the community in which your agency operates. You need to place your newsletter on the mailing lists of the programs, clubs, organizations, churches, businesses, and individuals in the community. By doing so, you offer them a means—your newsletter—by which they can publicize news and information that is important to them. They will provide a source of news and information as well as the beginning of a mailing list with which you can build the circulation of your newsletter.

If you tap these three sources of information—the newspapers, your agency, and the community—you should have more material than you need for each issue of your newsletter. It's your responsibility to evaluate all of this material. Before you begin the actual layout and paste-up of an issue, divide all your material into three piles. In the first pile, place those news items that *absolutely must* appear in that issue of the newsletter. In the second pile, place those items that could be printed in the next issue. Any remaining material belongs in the third pile—your "newsletter fillers." At this point, you are ready to begin the layout and paste-up of your newsletter.

PUTTING YOUR NEWSLETTER TO BED

You will need to complete the following tasks in preparing your newsletter for the printer: lay out and paste up the masthead and column heads, place advertisements in appropriate spaces, edit news briefs, write major news stories, place fillers, and proofread the final copy. Each of these tasks, and the order in which you complete them, is essential. In the following sections, we will discuss these tasks in detail.

LAY OUT AND PASTE UP THE MASTHEAD AND COLUMN HEADS

Your masthead should include the name of your newsletter, your agency's logo, and the volume and number of the issue. The name and logo, which remain unchanged, help your newsletter to build a circulation and gain recognition in the community. The volume and number are needed to make your newsletter a part of the public record. Since your masthead will distinguish your newsletter from others, it should be attractive enough to project a positive image of your agency. You can add other items to your masthead that will increase the exposure and visibility of your newsletter and your agency. For example, you might include your agency's mailing address and phone number (including zip and area codes), the circulation of the previous issue, or a brief quotation (especially one that is identified with your agency).

Although column heads may or may not appear regularly in your newsletter, we strongly recommend that you develop regular and predictable sections in your newsletter. If a certain feature appears in every issue, its location within the newsletter shouldn't be changed. This predictability of placement will allow you to paste up the column heads for these sections. This is also the time to paste up page numbers if they are to be used.

PLACE ADVERTISEMENTS IN APPROPRIATE SPACES

If your agency is on a shoestring budget, advertising may be the only way in which you can subsidize a newsletter (unless there is a group of individuals who will underwrite the costs of production and printing). You should allot no more than 50% of your space to advertisements. Otherwise, your newsletter will become an advertising supplement in which the publicity you originally intended to give your agency will be overshadowed.

Before you begin to solicit advertising for your newsletter, you need to determine specific advertising rates. (Also, if you intend to do the layout and design of your ads, you must establish a specific charge for these services.) In order to determine your advertising rates, you need to calculate the cost of circulating, producing, and printing each issue of your newsletter. Circulation can be accomplished through a distribution system staffed by volunteers. Production costs, which cover primarily the expense involved in purchasing basic materials, shouldn't affect the cost of every issue. Printing costs, therefore, should be the overwhelming consideration when you compute advertising rates for your newsletter. Your printing costs will be determined by the number of pages in your newsletter and the number of copies printed.

Once you've established advertising rates, you should be able to sell space in your newsletter: potential advertisers are almost unlimited. It's a question of knowing where to look. Ask yourself the following questions: How many small businesses are located in our community? Which businesses does our agency employ for services? What community-based, human-service agencies are similar to ours? What are the sources of news and information for our newsletter? How many churches are there in our community? How many schools? There are people in each of these organizations who have reasons to advertise in your newsletter. Your job is to tell them why *your* newsletter should publicize their message.

Advertising shouldn't appear on the front page of your newsletter. The purpose of the front page is to attract attention and invite the potential reader to examine your newsletter. Advertisements should be distributed throughout an issue. Your goal is to evenly distribute and balance as many ads as possible. Unless you have previously agreed to a special arrangement, you should place your ads at the bottom of the page, or in the inside columns.

Two very different situations may arise with regard to advertising space. If you've sold mostly quarter-page and full-page ads in one issue and you're not planning to use the bottom of the back page for mailing purposes, a full-page ad should be placed on the last page. If that's impossible, a full-page ad should be placed on the inside cover of either the second page or the next-to-the-last page of the newsletter. (Full-page ads must always be pasted up first.)

The other possibility is that you may have to place a large number of small ads in one issue. A number of such ads might be used in the middle of your newsletter to provide an attractive border around community news items. Whether or not such a layout design is practical for your publication, your goal is to balance and distribute small ads throughout your newsletter.

Since a perfect balance is rare, the final unfilled page is dealt with last in layout and paste-up. In order to resolve the competition for space that exists between advertising and information on this page, you should return to your newsletter departments to determine how much space these departments still have for advertisements. If a particular department contains less material than usual in an issue, there may be more space available in which you can place small ads. Likewise, when a department contains more material than usual, several small ads may have to be moved. As the producer of a newsletter, you will be faced with situations in which either advertising must be excluded or material must be edited. In such a situation, you should always edit material, deleting *everything* that is redundant or unnecessary.

When you place a full-page ad on the last page of your newsletter, the next-to-the-last page becomes the "garbage page." On other pages of a newsletter, the ads are balanced in size and number, but the layout on the "garbage page" isn't subject to the standards and rules that apply to other pages.

Once the advertisements have been pasted up, there should be no need to move any of the ads or alter their arrangement. (This does not apply to the "garbage page.") At this stage, it is unwise to accept late ads—ads that come in after your advertising deadline has passed.

EDIT NEWS BRIEFS

When you edit news briefs, you are dealing with the most difficult and critical step in the production process—a step that involves some reviewing and rewriting of the news items you've placed in the "must appear" pile of material.

In carrying out this step, you need to be able to recognize the essential information in any news item.

When you're ready to lay out your news briefs, the following suggestions might be helpful. Use columns that are two inches wide or less. Never continue a news brief from one column to another. Try to place your most important news briefs at the top of the page. Give each news brief a short title and let the title stand out from the news brief itself. Review each news brief and delete unnecessary words and sentences. Finally, try various arrangements of the news briefs before you decide which layout design you'll use.

Small spaces can be left for brief inserts. Leaving such space, however, is not necessary or mandatory. The only spaces that should be left are those that are too small to fill with other short news briefs. It is imperative that no regular column be left totally blank; if nothing else is available, a brief quote will suffice.

WRITE MAJOR NEWS STORIES

The stories you write for the front page of your newsletter should be major articles about issues and subjects of concern to your agency and the community in which it operates. Only a story of great significance should cover the entire front page.

The front page of your newsletter should invite people to pick it up and read it—it should attract the attention of browsers. Since you want to attract the attention of as many people as possible, your front page should cover a number of topics.

The front page should be laid out first for two reasons: (1) to determine if there will be any front-page space left (a small space should be left if at all possible), and (2) no remaining page should be laid out before you know whether or not anything will have to be continued from the front page.

A number of front-page designs are available. (You should choose a design before you begin to lay out the front page.) For example, you might decide to divide the page into two or three columns and run one story across the top half of the page.

It's best to write and type up news stories before you write the headlines for them: the length of a story dictates the size of the lettering to be used in the headline. When you write news stories, present only the facts, and present them in the order of their importance. When you write features, focus on what or who is involved in your story. Use the names of the individuals involved. One of the fundamentals of journalism states that the names of local people will attract the attention of readers in the community. When you write your own opinions, explain your topic, your opinion, and your reasons for holding that opinion.

Whenever you write a story for your newsletter, write in a tone and style your readers can identify with and understand.

PLACE FILLERS

Fillers are those items that appear in every issue of a newsletter but vary in location from issue to issue.

Before you begin the task of placing fillers, separate those pages that are completely filled from those that contain empty space. Set aside the completed pages, since they won't be needed until you proofread all the pages before sending them to the printer.

You are now ready to focus on those pages that contain unfilled spaces. At this point, arrange your mandatory fillers according to size. Begin with the largest filler and find space for it. Then find space for the next filler, and so on. Repeat this procedure until every mandatory filler has been used. If you run out of space before you run out of fillers, your editorial skills must come into play again. You need to be able to decide if an article can be shortened or a news brief can be eliminated.

At times, there may be spaces that are too small for any of your mandatory fillers; for example, you could use a small reproduction of your agency's logo or motto. You should keep a folder for fillers of different sizes or designs that could be used in small spaces. Items such as drawings, magazine reproductions, and interesting facts could be kept in the folder.

PROOFREAD THE FINAL COPY

When you've filled the last empty space, the layout and paste-up are finished. Now you must proofread your work. Look for distracting blank spaces and crooked lines. Then, as you read the final copy, look for grammatical errors, misspellings, and unclear sentences. You should also make sure that names, addresses, and phone numbers are correct. Once proofread, your newsletter is ready for the printer.

HOW TO BUILD THE CIRCULATION
OF YOUR NEWSLETTER

Once you've decided to "construct" a newsletter, you'll need to develop a list of potential subscribers. Your advertisers should appear at the top of this list. Send each of them a copy of your newsletter so that they can see their ads in print. You should also include the names of people who provide financial, media, and public support for your agency. Add to that list the names of the clients your agency serves. Then list your sources of news and information. Next, develop a list of people in television, radio, and newspapers, potential funding sources, and public (political) figures. Remember, every member of the community is a potential reader or subscriber.

HOW TO EVALUATE YOUR NEWSLETTER

When your newsletter is returned from the printer, you should ask yourself how you feel about the final and finished copy. Do you see any errors? What do you wish you'd done differently? What will you delete in future issues? What do you think, in terms of content and design, merits repeated use? What are the strengths of your newsletter? What are its weaknesses? When you answer these questions, you should be your own worst critic. In other words, don't be satisfied with anything that could have been better. Accept no excuses and make no excuses for yourself. This self-critique will help you to anticipate and deal with criticism from others.

Examine your readers' suggestions and weigh their validity. Above all, thank them for caring enough to have read your newsletter. Their feedback helps you to determine how your publication is being received. Listen attentively to negative as well as positive reactions—reactions that will help you to understand what you overlooked, what you explained, what you overstated, what you made clear, and why you did the things you did.

SUMMARY

A good newsletter can serve a variety of purposes for your agency. It can be a source of information, opinions, and announcements, can help raise funds, and can create a sense of community consciousness.

You don't have to be an expert in media to develop an attractively designed and informative newsletter. You do need, however, certain basic materials and equipment and an understanding of the sequential steps involved in developing a quality newsletter. The purpose of this chapter has been to outline those steps.

The gathering of materials and equipment and mastery of the production steps are easy to accomplish, but they do not guarantee a quality newsletter. The value of particular stories and the visual image created by the arrangement of articles on a page are insights that you will gain as you acquire experience. Following the suggestions in this chapter will give you a headstart in developing an outstanding newsletter for your agency.

SUGGESTED REFERENCES

MacDougall, C. *Interpretative reporting.* New York: Macmillan Publishing Co., Inc., 1977. This is one of the best introductions to journalism. It explains how the world of journalism operates and discusses various kinds of news writing. The book also explains how to approach a variety of writing assignments.

The following introductory works offer similar information:

Crump, S. *Fundamentals of journalism.* New York: McGraw-Hill Book Company, 1974.

Hough, G. A. *News writing.* Boston: Houghton Mifflin Co., 1975.

Hill, E., and Breen, J. J. *Reporting and writing the news.* Boston: Little, Brown and Co., 1977.

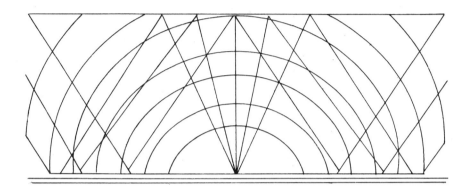

USING PRESS RELEASES AND THE BROADCAST MEDIA

Bonita Trumbule
Gerald Trumbule

CHAPTER 7

"At times, it seems as though small community-based, social-service agencies come and go so fast that their efforts could not possibly be felt. But this is not so. These agencies are going through a unique process of evolution. Each one stands on the shoulders of its predecessors, learning from mistakes as well as successes. A real spirit of cooperation and sharing is growing among these agencies. As long as there are people who truly care, small social-service agencies will survive."

In 1972, Bonita and Gerald Trumbule established a small nonprofit organization in Denver. Since that time, their organization has grown and prospered, and the programs it offers have changed and evolved to serve the needs of the community.

We will consider the following questions in this chapter:

How can you create public awareness of your agency?
What channels of communication are open to community organizations?
How can you publicize on a low budget?
Should your agency use newspapers, television, or radio?
How and when should you write a press release?
How can you produce a public-service announcement (PSA)?

INTRODUCTION

Publicity is critical to the effective operation of most small community-based, social-service agencies. It's difficult to serve a community whose members are unaware of your agency's existence. If you fail to establish contact with the public, your agency will fail to accomplish its task. How, then, can the community be made aware of your agency and the services it can provide? The purpose of this chapter is to provide you with some practical advice on how to publicize your agency.

PLANNING YOUR PUBLICITY

Before you begin to publicize your organization, you need to decide on the intent, or purpose, of the publicity. It is extremely important to be clear in your own mind about the purpose of your publicity if you expect the message to be clear to the public. You might want to publicize information concerning the services your agency provides, or you might want to instigate specific action to meet the needs of the community.

After you've determined the purpose of your publicity, you need to assess the capabilities of your organization. Ask yourself the following questions: How much money can our organization afford to spend? How much time can we invest in publicity? What are the capabilities of our staff? How much publicity does our organization need? How frequently do we need to publicize? (Once a year? Once a month?) Should we develop a "one-shot" media event or a continuing publicity campaign?

REACHING THE PUBLIC

Trying to reach the general public is like trying to make contact with a reclusive turtle. You can tap on its thick shell with a stick for months before the animal notices you. However, if you use publicity effectively, eventually you'll hear people say "Oh yeah, I've heard of your organization. What exactly do you people do over there?" instead of the usual "I didn't even know your organization existed."

The speed with which the public takes notice of your organization is directly related to the amount of information you provide in your publicity. A continuous publicity campaign will accelerate the awareness process, but it will also require a continuous effort on your part. An ongoing series of messages will make the public aware of the fact that your agency is alive and active. A single article or television spot will reach some people but in the overall picture will not create significant awareness.

THREE CHANNELS OF COMMUNICATION

Generally speaking, there are three channels of communication through which your organization can reach potential clients: word of mouth (or direct human contact), newspapers, and the electronic broadcast media of radio and television.

WORD OF MOUTH

The oldest and most well known channel of communication is direct human contact, or word of mouth. Even if you choose to use more sophisticated forms of communication, the things people tell one another about your agency (formally or informally) will affect the performance of your organization and determine its reputation. You should be aware of what people think, feel, and say about your organization, and use other channels of communication to modify, redirect, or amplify their feelings.

NEWSPAPERS

For our purposes, our discussion of the medium of print will be limited to the development of press releases. Flyers, brochures, posters, and newsletters are covered in other chapters.

PRESS RELEASES

Press releases are used to generate the flow of information. A press release must convey the information you want to communicate in a clear, concise manner that will survive the newspaper editor's blue pencil. The amount of copy used in a press release is often determined by the space that is available rather than the content of the article. Therefore, you need to place all pertinent information in the first few paragraphs of your release and then reiterate and expand on that information in subsequent paragraphs. Keep your sentence structure simple and your information direct. Don't expect the editor of the newspaper to rewrite your article. A picture is worth at least a thousand words, and it will attract the reader's eye. If you decide to include a photograph, remember that glossy, low-contrast, black-and-white action photos are most effective.

If you look in your city's telephone directory, you'll probably find the names of newspapers you were unaware of in the past. Don't hesitate to send your press release to *all* the newspapers listed. It's better to send information where it's not needed than not to send it where it is needed. You should develop a mailing list for your news releases—a master list of the addresses of newspapers, newsletters, and individuals who can "spread the word." These addresses can be transferred onto pregummed labels. This will save an enormous amount of time if you send out releases on a regular basis.

The following example of a press release illustrates the points we've discussed here concerning form and style.

MEDIA RELEASE

From: COMMUNITY FILM: a program of SEBASTIAN HOUSE, INC.
      1629 York St., Denver, 80206
Contact: JERRY TRUMBULE, DIRECTOR (Telephone: 321-2743)
Re: COMMUNITY FILM RECEIVES COLORADO COUNCIL GRANT

COMMUNITY FILM RECEIVES COLORADO COUNCIL GRANT

Community Film, a program of Sebastian House, Inc., announced the receipt of a matching grant of $2000 from the Colorado Council on the Arts and Humanities. Gerald H. Trumbule, independent filmmaker and Director of Community Film, said that the funds, which come in part from the National Endowment for the Arts and in part from the Colorado General Assembly, will be used to upgrade The Film School, an ongoing instructional program.

The Film School, located at 1629 York Street in Denver, has offered classes to the public in film, video, and related topics for the past three years. Over 400 students have taken 35 courses from 19 staff artists. Classes range from the simple (making better home movies) to the technical (editing sync-sound in 16mm).

According to Trumbule, programs of this sort at a community level are rather unusual. Due to the large investment that is needed in equipment and materials, most classes in filmmaking are offered by large universities. Community Film strives to keep the cost of learning about filmmaking and production at a minimum. Grants such as the one received from the Colorado Council, donations from local businesses such as IBM and Western Cine, and the contributions of time and effort made by local artists have made The Film School program possible. Denver is the only city in the Rocky Mountain region to have such a school.

In addition to enrolling in the many classes offered at the Film School, serious students of film can opt for membership or apprenticeship status and take part in programs that offer a shortcut to independent film production for the highly motivated. One former participant, Mike Speaker, was a winner of last year's regional Academy Award in the category of animation, and he is now working in Hollywood.

Community Film also offers media services to other nonprofit organizations. By applying the energies of advanced students to the needs of these organizations, Community Film produces low-cost film work and maintains quality while the students gain valuable experience. Local community organizations avail themselves of these services for the production of public-service announcements, fund-raising promotions, and documentaries about their programs. For example, a 30-minute documentary on child care was recently completed for the University of Colorado Medical Center. The documentary was produced at about half the cost of commercial production.

You can keep information about your agency flowing by sending out news releases regularly. Small newspapers usually need copy; if your releases are well written, they will be used. Larger metropolitan newspapers are often more difficult to crack, but, by establishing a personal contact with the reporter or editor who covers your type of agency, you can enhance your efforts. Whenever possible, you should make an appointment to deliver your news release in person in order to discuss it and answer any questions that might arise. If your news release contains information regarding a specific date or event, you should give the newspapers at least one month's lead time.

THE BROADCAST MEDIA

The electronic broadcast media of radio and television are the best means of reaching today's public. Most people avail themselves of one or both of these channels of communication every day. A community-service organization can publicize its message through the broadcast media by using advertisements.

ADVERTISEMENTS

Advertisements, which usually involve purchased air time, are produced by professional advertising agencies. When you hire an agency to produce your advertisement, and then buy air time for the finished product, you ensure the professional quality of your message and maintain control over the exact time at which it will be aired; however, the overriding consideration when you employ advertising agencies is cost. Production companies may charge as much as $2500 to develop and produce a thirty-second ad. If your budget allows for such an expense, this is one way to go. Most community-service organizations don't have enough money to employ agencies, and, therefore, they have to develop their own advertising.

MEDIA EVENTS

A media event is a staged occurrence that attracts the attention of the representatives of the broadcast media. The primary advantage involved in the use of media events is that your agency doesn't have to pay for production or air time. On the other hand, media events are very time consuming. A lot of work is involved in staging an event that is so compelling that news teams will flock to your door. Also, you may lose control of your message in the midst of the event. A reporter's individual interpretation of your event and delivery of your story might not convey your intended message. You can't always count on the news media to go along with your great idea; and to get them to agree to come to your event, you have to make arrangements well in advance (or hope for a slow news day).

PUBLIC-SERVICE ANNOUNCEMENTS

Radio and television stations provide free air time for public-service announcements, which are produced by the organizations they publicize. Public-service announcements are inexpensive. According to Federal Communications Commission guidelines, the media must make air time available to nonprofit organizations at no charge. Also, radio and television stations frequently make their recording time available to such organizations. When you use public-service announcements, you retain control of your message (providing, of course, that you don't slander anyone or use any four-letter words).

The only disadvantage involved when you use public-service announcements is that you're at the mercy of radio and television stations; they'll play your message at *their* chosen time and frequency. (This is particularly true in large cities.) Have you ever noticed that most public-service announcements are aired between 2:00 A.M. and 6:00 A.M.? Often, a message that you had hoped would be aired many times is played once or twice and then shelved.

STEPS INVOLVED IN PRODUCING PUBLIC-SERVICE ANNOUNCEMENTS

In order to improve the quality and effectiveness of your public-service announcements, you need to determine the purpose of your message, decide which medium to use, and prepare your message carefully. We will now discuss each of these three steps in detail.

Determine the Purpose of Your Message. What do you want to say to the public? Do you want to make them aware of your organization? If so, you should develop a series of messages or a campaign in which certain themes are repeated in order to reinforce the public's awareness of your agency. You might want to start out by informing the public of the problem your agency is attempting to solve, and then provide information about the agency itself. If your agency has been in existence for a long time and you feel that the public is already aware of it, you might want to think of a new slant or a fresh approach to your announcement. For example, you could emphasize the services your agency provides by highlighting the success story of one of your clients or by actually using a client in the message.

If you want to recruit volunteers, you should stress the importance and rewards of volunteerism rather than seek volunteers for your specific agency. You might want to publicize a very simple message concerning an upcoming event that your organization is sponsoring. In this case, be sure to include all vital information in your message—the name of the event, the date, the place, the time, and your agency's name and phone number.

Decide Which Medium to Use. Once you've determined the purpose of your message, you need to decide which medium to use. Would radio be as effective as television? When you stick to radio, your production tasks are relatively simple. Television adds the visual dimension and, for this reason, is usually more effective. When you want to reach as many people as possible, the best approach is to use both radio *and* television.

At this point, you should consider the audience you are attempting to reach with your message. Most television stations are directed at the general public. Stations that broadcast on PBS—the Public Broadcasting Service— direct their programming at an educated audience. Different radio stations attract different audiences. There are soul stations, rock stations, classical stations, news stations, and others. The medium you employ and the particular station you choose will be determined by the purpose and content of your message.

Prepare Your Message Carefully. Make some notes concerning what you want to say. Your message should be clear, concise, and simple. Read it to someone who might be able to give you fresh insight as well as criticism. After you've written your message, you need to time it by reading it while someone clocks it with a stopwatch. Standard lengths for public-service announcements are 10, 20, 30, and 60 seconds, but the 30-second announcement is preferable.

When you're satisfied with the message you've written, type it clearly and list the name, address, and telephone number of your agency at the top of the page along with the name of a contact person within your agency and the dates for the announcement of your message. You should send your message at least two weeks before you would like it to be aired.

EXAMPLES OF RADIO PSAs

The following example of a public-service announcement is a 20-second spot that was written and produced by members of an organization to recruit volunteers:

Make a difference in someone's life—volunteer . . . at a hospital, a neighborhood center, a community school. Call one of them, or call us at 573-8888.
That's the Mile High Community Center—573-8888.

Our second example of a public-service announcement is a 30-second spot
produced by a coalition of alternative schools. Its purpose was to make the
public aware of alternative education and of a referral service from which more
information about specific alternative schools could be obtained:

Twelve thousand hours! That's how much time a young person spends in
school from first grade through high school graduation. Those hours can
be very long if you're not enjoying them. There are schools in which learning is fun—where you help decide what you'll learn. The Alternative
Learning Coalition can refer you to such schools. For more information,
call 366-7656.

TELEVISION PSAs

Unless you've worked in front of a television camera in the past, you
shouldn't try to read your message on camera. Usually, it's most practical to
use either 35 mm color slides or 16mm motion picture film in the production of
your PSA. Most television stations accept slides and then transfer them to videotape.

You can be very creative in your use of slides. You can show your organization at work, illustrate an existing social problem, or demonstrate possible
solutions to specific problems. When you use slides that are visually exciting and
attractive, you elicit a positive reaction from your audience. Your purpose and
intended message should be enhanced and clarified by your slides. They should
relate directly to your printed copy. Don't show beautiful scenes of the moun-
tains when you are talking about the problems of alcoholism. A good rule to
follow when you take slides for PSAs is to avoid the alienated medium and the
long shot. If you get close to the action, you'll find that your slides are more
compelling. Perhaps your organization has access to slides that could be used in
your PSA. Ask around. If none are available, you'll have to produce some. If
you can't do it yourself, find someone who can do it for you: another staff
person, a friend, or a member of the board of directors.

After you've decided which slides to use, number them according to the
order in which they will be used in the finished production. Each slide should
correspond to a specific portion of your written copy.

Now you're ready to prepare your PSA for delivery to a television station.
Type your copy (the verbal portion of your PSA) on a page headed by your
agency's name, address, and telephone number, along with the name of a contact
person within your agency and the dates on which your message should be

aired. Remember to give television stations enough lead time to get your message on the air. A month is usually ample. In the left-hand margin of the copy, list the slides as they are to be shown.

The following example of a slide/copy script illustrates the form in which your PSA should appear.

16 February 1978

Script for a 30-second PSA
for
University Year for Action
Metropolitan State College
Contact person: Bob Clifton, 629-3267

SCRIPT

PICTURE	SOUND
A series of rapid dissolves:	(Voice-over narration)
Slide #1, dissolve to #2,	Everybody knows we've got problems.
Dissolve to	
Slide #3, dissolve to	But what can one person do about them?
Slide #4, dissolve to	You can get involved,
Slide #5, dissolve to	help others,
Slide #6, dissolve to	and earn college credits for yourself.
Slide #7, dissolve to	The Center for Community Services
Slide #8, dissolve to	at Metropolitan State College
Slide #9, dissolve to	has a community-action program for you.
Slide #10	
Dissolve to Slide #11,	Get involved.
and hold for vidifont.	(vidifont)
	University Year for Action
	Call 629-3267

You will need 5 to 15 slides for a 30-second PSA. Your message and theme will help to determine exactly how many slides you will need. If your message moves slowly and is intended to have a serious and somber effect, you'll need few slides. If you want to convey a feeling of action in your message, you'll need more slides. You should cut from slide to slide if you want snappy, quick action. On the other hand, a dissolve—the overlapping fade out of one slide and fade in of the next—produces a softer effect.

If you want your PSA to be aired on all the stations in your area, you usually have to go to only one station. The staff at that station will transfer your slides to videotape and provide a narrator for your script. (Although you may do the narration yourself if you wish, television stations can provide professionals.) Then, you have to find out the date on which your PSA is to be produced, call the other television stations, and ask them to send videotape to the producing station in advance of that date. The station will then transfer a copy of your PSA to as many reels of videotape as you have arranged to have sent to them and send the taped copies to the other stations for airing.

Large advertisers use film instead of slides, because film is exciting, creative, and effective. Movies move people. Small social-service agencies, however, need to consider the costs involved in the use of film. A 16mm PSA will cost a minimum of $100 to $150 for materials alone. If you've decided to use film for your PSA but you can't persuade a professional filmmaker to donate time to your agency and you have no filmmakers on your staff, you should contact film schools and film departments of universities in your area. Often, students of film will work without pay in order to gain the experience they need. Before you agree to involve students in your project, you should examine their previous work, or sample reels, in order to get an idea of how accomplished they are.

A detailed discussion of the complicated mechanics involved in producing a 16mm PSA is not within the scope of this book; however, if your agency can afford to produce a 16mm PSA, then this is obviously the best way to go. Beautifully executed film spots receive an extraordinary amount of air time. One such spot, done for a Native American organization in the Denver area, combined the beauty of full-dress Indian dance and music with exciting color and camera work. The spot was played over 200 times, without charge, by the three local television stations (often during prime time).

FURTHER TIPS

You should keep two things in mind after your PSA has been aired. First, always keep copies of PSAs that have been aired over television or radio. These copies will prove invaluable in the production of future PSAs. Second, it pays to stay on the good side of the broadcast media. A letter thanking them for their help in publicizing your message will be greatly appreciated and, as a matter of fact, will help them to keep their license.

SUMMARY

Publicity is absolutely essential to the effectiveness of any community-service organization. In order to reach the public, your agency needs to maintain a flow of information. Write and send out press releases regularly. Publicize every newsworthy event and development that takes place in your organization: the initiation of new projects, the receipt of grants, the recruitment of new personnel, the appointment of new members to the board of directors, and so on.

Radio and television spots are extremely effective. Learn how to produce PSAs and keep them flowing. Develop a working relationship with the members of the local press and the public affairs directors of local television and radio stations.

Become familiar with all the channels of communication that are available to you and use them. Your agency will prosper from your efforts, and you might even have a good time in the process!

SUGGESTED REFERENCES

Bobker, L. R. *Making movies from script to screen.* New York: Harcourt, Brace Jovanovich, Inc., 1973. A handbook that is appropriate for students or for those who simply want to become acquainted with 16mm production.

McLuhan, M. *The medium is the message.* New York: Bantam Books, 1967. This book provides a look at the ways in which the media affect us in our daily lives.

Woolley, A. E. *Creative 35mm techniques.* New York: American Photographic Book Publishing Company, Inc., 1963. A book that explains how to get in there and capture the action with interesting, compelling photographs.

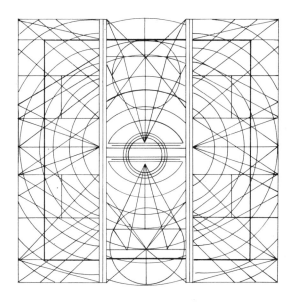

VOLUNTEER
SUPPORT
SYSTEMS
PART THREE

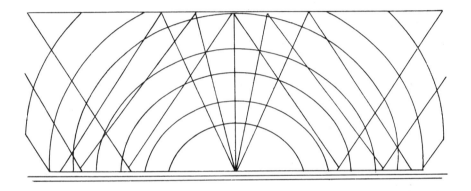

EFFECTIVE VOLUNTEER PROGRAMS

Marlene Wilson

CHAPTER 8

"As communities become more diverse and complex, so do their problems. In my opinion, the small social-service agency is in a unique position to both identify and respond to the needs of the local community. Such agencies are able to match available resources to real needs as those needs are identified by those who experience them."

While she was the director of a voluntary-action center, Marlene Wilson worked closely with a wide variety of community agencies. She blends this experience with the knowledge she gained in personnel administration in her very popular book, *The Effective Management of Volunteer Programs.*

We will consider the following questions in this chapter:

Who needs volunteers?
By using volunteers, does an agency get something for nothing?
Who should run volunteer programs?
How are volunteers recruited?

ATTITUDES TOWARD VOLUNTEERS

Administrators of small community-based, social-service agencies are frequently faced with a crucial decision: whether or not to use volunteers. There are a number of compelling reasons for using volunteers:

1. Volunteers can improve an agency's community image.
2. Some funding sources (public, as well as private) insist on citizen involvement.
3. Paid staff members are often overworked and frustrated.
4. Volunteers bring added dimensions to services for clients (such as unhurried attention, one-to-one caring, and community input in planning).

On the other hand, skeptics maintain that:

1. Volunteers are not professional and are, therefore, untrustworthy regarding confidentiality and reliability.
2. Volunteers bring added dimensions to services for clients (such as
3. unhurried attention, one-to-one caring, and community input in planning).

It is important that you weigh these pros and cons carefully before you decide whether or not volunteers are both needed and wanted in your agency. The material in this chapter is not intended to convince you of the value of volunteer programs. It is meant to suggest how a volunteer program might be administered effectively once the decision to have one has been made.

The key to a successful volunteer program is the administrator's attitude toward it. Experience has shown that, when agency administrators are either unsupportive or neutral in their attitude toward volunteer programs, the programs are almost always fraught with problems. The notion that the program is not really important inevitably spreads to the staff and is picked up by the volunteers. The tension between the staff members and the volunteers mounts, and the quality of their work suffers.

On the other hand, if the head of a program believes in the importance of volunteers as "unpaid staff"—that is, as invaluable members of the agency's team —then a climate of acceptance, mutual respect, and support can be established. When that climate prevails, and the paid staff members and volunteers see themselves as members of one group, a healthy, give-and-take relationship results. Since their attitudes are important to the success of volunteer programs, administrators need to examine their feelings about volunteers *before* they incorporate any into their organizations.

As an administrator of a social-service agency, you could determine your attitude toward volunteers by answering the following questions: Have you hired someone or will you hire someone to direct the volunteer component of your agency? Or is this assignment handed around in a haphazard fashion to whichever staff member has the lightest load? Is it assumed that the director of volunteers will take on the responsibilities of that position on a part-time basis while he or she continues to carry out other assignments?

Frequently, qualifications for the position of volunteer director aren't specified, and, after a person has been given the assignment, little (if any) training is provided to prepare him or her for the job. Moreover, the salary paid to a director of volunteers often reflects the notion that that person should be willing to donate much of his or her time. As a result, it is sometimes difficult to ascertain whether this assignment should be regarded as a promotion or a demotion. Only you, as the administrator, can deal effectively with this situation. Your actions will convey your attitude to all concerned.

THE DIRECTOR OF VOLUNTEERS

The director of volunteers is an important element in the successful involvement of volunteers. This position has evolved during the past few years into one of the most important influences on the human-services scene, and it should be given careful attention. These directors need to be skilled administrators. The work force they manage is part-time, unpaid, and assigned to perform a variety of tasks. Volunteer directors need to be aware of the following developments affecting volunteerism today: changes in the makeup of the volunteer work force have taken place, there is a growing demand for volunteers, opposition to volunteerism has surfaced, and public attention is focused on citizen involvement.

Changes in the Makeup of the Volunteer Work Force. Contrary to a widely held belief that volunteerism is dying, the ACTION survey conducted by the Census Bureau, entitled *Americans Volunteer—1974,* indicated that approximately 37 million people in the U.S. volunteered during that year—that is, one of every five persons over the age of 14. Other knowledgeable sources estimate that figure to be over 50 million. There have been some interesting changes in the makeup of this volunteer work force:

1. Almost half (41%) are men.
2. Fewer women between the ages of 25 and 55 (often regarded as the "traditional volunteer") are involved as volunteers.
3. More students (both high school and college) are volunteering in order to gain valid learning experiences.
4. Steadily growing numbers of persons over 60 years of age, responding through programs that have removed barriers such as out-of-pocket expenses and transportation, are seeking to help and to share their experience and wisdom with others.
5. Rapidly increasing numbers of working people who feel dissatisfied or unfulfilled in their jobs are coming to volunteerism to add a new dimension to their lives.
6. More clients are serving as helpers as well as helpees.

These changes make for a richly varied, greatly diverse work force that is available to agencies willing and able to provide growth, opportunities to learn, meaningful jobs, and valid supervision and recognition.

There is a Growing Demand for Volunteers. This means that there is a competitive market; the prospective volunteer has a veritable smorgasbord of options. Today's volunteers are very discerning—they won't stay with poorly organized programs.

Opposition to Volunteerism Has Surfaced. The National Organization for Women (NOW) has spoken out against service volunteering, claiming that it exploits women. Some professional unions have eyed volunteerism suspiciously, especially during periods of economic recession. When paid staff is cut, they ask whether agencies are, in fact, replacing paid staff with volunteers.

Public Attention Is Focused on Citizen Involvement. National advertising and magazine articles have brought volunteerism before the public as never before.

An effective director of volunteers, then, is someone who can manage a work force made up of both men and women, ranging in age from teenager to retiree, with a wide range of education, skills, and degree of professionalism. And this work force is part-time, working throughout the agency on varied time schedules.

Volunteer programs (if they are to succeed) *do* cost something:

1. Administrative commitment and support.
2. Money to support the office of volunteers and to hire a competent director.
3. Staff time to help plan the program, design the jobs, and train and supervise the volunteers.

We've begun with a picture of the realities involved in operating volunteer programs, because we feel that a misunderstanding of these programs has created two kinds of problems that confront volunteer involvement in organizations today: (1) problems between staff members and volunteers, and (2) problems between staff members and board members. (Don't forget that board members are volunteers.)

THE FUNCTIONS OF THE DIRECTOR

The position of director of volunteers is a management position. All the functions of a manager must be performed by a director of volunteers in a logical sequence. A widely accepted definition of the term *manager* is "someone who works with and through others to accomplish organizational goals." In his book, *The Practice of Management,* Peter Drucker (1954) states "A Manager does his work by getting other people to do theirs."

Since the directors of volunteer programs work with and through others (both paid and unpaid staff members) to accomplish goals, they are, and must be considered, managers. Their functions include planning, organizing, staffing, directing, and controlling. In *The Effective Management of Volunteer Programs* (Wilson, 1976), these functions are reviewed and translated into terminology frequently used in working with volunteers (see Figure 8-1).

We will now examine these functions as they relate to the director of a volunteer program.

PLANNING GOALS, OBJECTIVES, AND ACTIVITIES

It's essential that plans be completed *before* volunteers are recruited and that all parties affected by volunteer involvement—the volunteer director, paid staff members, volunteers, clients, and administration— have representation on the planning groups. This is one of the most effective ways of avoiding, or at least minimizing, staff resistance.

The three major steps in the planning process involve: (1) goals, (2) objectives, and (3) action plans.

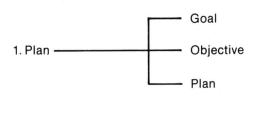

1. Plan ——————— Goal
                 Objective
                 Plan

2. Organize ——————— Job Design

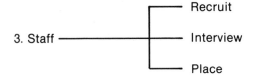

3. Staff ——————— Recruit
                 Interview
                 Place

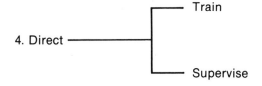

4. Direct ——————— Train
                 Supervise

5. Control ——————— Evaluate

FIGURE 8-1. The Functions of a Manager.

The first thing an organization or agency needs to do in the planning process is identify and clearly state its purpose for being, or its mission (also referred to as its goal). The goal should be written in specific terms and shared with everyone who works with the agency. In this way, people can see how their individual jobs relate to the agency's overall purpose. This knowledge could make the difference between working toward a goal and just doing a job.

Once this "reason for being" has been defined, it is necessary to set *organizational objectives,* which are specific targets that will help staff members achieve the agency's overall goal. These objectives should be specific, measurable, achievable, and compatible with the agency's overall goal.

Finally, for each objective, the members of the agency need to develop a clearly written *plan of action* to determine: (1) who will achieve the objective, (2) when the work will be done, (3) how it will be accomplished, and (4) how much money will be required to implement the objective.

This planning process helps everyone to accomplish the overall goal in an orderly fashion and feel a sense of commitment and a sense of success and reward when objectives are reached.

Joint planning sessions for volunteer programs are sometimes maintained on a permanent basis to provide ongoing problem solving and evaluation. Without careful planning, programs can flounder and waste the time and energy of both paid staff members and volunteers. Planning must be an ongoing, continuous process, because needs change, workers change, and the volunteer work force changes. Agency members must be aware of and responsive to these changes.

ORGANIZING THE JOB DESIGN

After the members of the planning group have determined the objectives of the volunteer program, they need to design and organize the jobs (both volunteer and paid) that will enable them to achieve those objectives. At this point, the planning group should decide which jobs should be done by paid staff members and which ones should be performed by volunteers.

In the past, volunteer work assignments were often made haphazardly and job descriptions for volunteer work were rarely written: confusion was inevitable. Today, the need for job descriptions is almost universally recognized. The following is an example of a job description for a volunteer position.

Title: Speaker's Bureau Coordinator
Responsible to: Director of Volunteers (or Public Relations Supervisor)
Definition of Duties: Give presentations and addresses on behalf of this agency for the purpose of recruiting volunteers and encouraging community support of our organization and its goals. Addresses are to be given at service clubs, churches, and other locations as assigned.
Time Required: Four to six hours per month.

Qualifications: The ability to speak effectively before an audience and operate visual aid equipment. Also a commitment to this agency's goals and objectives, and a belief in the value of volunteers. Enthusiasm is a must.

Training Provided: Orientation sessions will be arranged with staff members and volunteers to thoroughly acquaint new volunteers with this agency, the volunteer program, and the needs of both.

Social-service agencies should develop volunteer opportunities with varying levels of responsibility, providing "career-ladder" possibilities for those volunteers who are interested in assuming increasing responsibility.

It's important to remember that volunteers, as well as paid staff members, are motivated by the work they do. In *Motivation and Organizational Climate* (Litwin & Stringer, 1968), several motivators are listed: achievement, recognition for accomplishment, challenging work, increased responsibility, and growth and development.

STAFFING, RECRUITING, INTERVIEWING, AND PLACING VOLUNTEERS

Once jobs have been clearly defined, and your agency knows exactly what it needs, recruitment and placement become productive and meaningful. At this point, your agency is able to "target recruit"—that is, to recruit individuals who have specific skills—rather than rely on a broad, general, "shotgun" approach. Moreover, when social-service agencies appeal to prospective volunteers to join their ranks by saying "we need you," the immediate response is "for what?" Those agencies that cannot answer this question will find it difficult to attract volunteers.

The following suggestions regarding the recruitment of volunteers should be helpful:

1. Do specific rather than general recruiting whenever possible.
2. Choose audiences whose interests and priorities relate to your needs.
3. Determine the skills you need and actively seek them out.
4. Establish a year-round recruitment plan.
5. Use a variety of recruitment techniques, such as newspaper ads, human-interest stories, radio and television spots, posters, billboards, bumper stickers, displays, tours and open houses, newsletters, and person-to-person contact.
6. Utilize the services of voluntary-action centers, volunteer bureaus, retired-senior volunteer programs, and student-volunteer bureaus.
7. Recruit volunteers from all segments of the community.

8. Be enthusiastic! If you, as a recruiter, aren't excited about your agency's programs, then those you attempt to recruit won't be excited.

When potential volunteers respond to your recruitment efforts, it is essential that they be carefully interviewed to determine their qualifications and personal attributes and to discover what they hope to derive from the volunteer assignment. Only when a recruiter and a potential volunteer share information about needs, expectations, job requirements, and goals is there a possibility of making a suitable match. During the interview, both the agency and the potential volunteer decide whether or not placement will be meaningful and satisfying.

TRAINING AND SUPERVISING

For our purposes, *training* refers to anything that helps to increase the realization of a person's or an organization's potential. (Behavioral scientists refer to training as *human-resource development.*) In establishing volunteer programs, it's important to train the volunteers, the staff members, and the director of volunteers.

Training Volunteers. New volunteers should go through a general orientation before they begin their training. During the orientation, information about an agency, its clients, procedures, and so on, is relayed to the new volunteers.

After the general orientation is completed, the training process begins, during which people grow and develop the skills and confidence they need to do their jobs well. The training provided should vary, depending on the job assignment and the background and experience of the volunteer. When in doubt, ask volunteers what they would like to know about their new jobs. (They will tell you!)

Paid staff members and experienced volunteers can be used to train new volunteers. This arrangement enhances team spirit and is an excellent means of recognition for the trainers.

Training Paid Staff Members. Before the first volunteers arrive, sessions should be held with staff members to discuss attitudes, techniques, and responsibilities, as well as the benefits to be derived from working with volunteers. The administrator's attitude toward volunteers is especially influential at this time.

If problems develop between staff members and volunteers in a program that is already in motion, the staff members must receive some training in the areas of problem solving and consciousness raising. Make no mistake—negative attitudes on the part of staff members have driven many volunteers away.

Training the Director of Volunteers. The director of volunteers should be encouraged to attend seminars and workshops that deal with the management of volunteers. The director also could attend courses in business management, sociology, psychology, communications, and adult education. This training should be encouraged and subsidized by your agency.

Supervising Volunteers. Supervision should be sensitive and humane, based on the philosophy of manager as "enabler of others." All volunteers should be supervised and should know to whom they are accountable. This may sound obvious, but one of the major complaints voiced by volunteers who leave agencies is "I never knew who I was accountable to or where I could bring ideas or problems. I never got any feedback as to whether or not I was doing well. As a result, I felt like I was operating in a vacuum." (It may be worth noting that this same complaint is voiced by paid staff members.)

Volunteers should be supervised by the person in charge of the project, area, ward, classroom, or program to which they have been assigned. One of the greatest fears of staff members is that they will lose control of the quality of the projects they are responsible for when volunteers become involved; however, this cannot happen when staff members supervise volunteers.

EVALUATING VOLUNTEER PROGRAMS

When volunteer programs are evaluated, all the affected parties represented in the planning process should be involved in the evaluation. It is important to conduct *objective* as well as *subjective* evaluations.

Objective evaluations measure the results of a program against its stated objectives and determine whether those objectives were met on schedule and within budget. If the program's goals and plans were clearly defined at the outset, evaluation becomes a simple process. Evaluators will be able to identify the things that were done correctly and the mistakes that were made, analyze this information, and feed the data into the planning process of the agency's next program.

Subjective evaluations determine how people *feel* about a program, its effectiveness, and its results. These evaluations involve the use of questionnaires, evaluation checklists, interviews, and group discussion sessions. (A series of evaluation checklists has been developed by the National Information Center on Volunteerism [P.O. Box 4179, Boulder, Colorado, 80306]. This series is called *Basic Feedback Systems* and is available at a minimal cost.)

When you conduct subjective evaluations, ask questions that relate to feelings and attitudes. The following questions are typical of those found in evaluation questionnaires:

1. What do you like about our present volunteer program?
2. What do you dislike about our program?
3. Are there things you would like to see changed in our volunteer program? (If so, please specify those changes.)
4. What volunteer jobs have you held in this agency? Which jobs have you found to be most satisfying and why? Which jobs were least

satisfying and why?

5. In your opinion, do paid staff members accept volunteers as team members? Do they resent volunteers?

6. In your opinion, how could we use volunteers more effectively in this agency?

Peter Drucker (1974) provides some helpful guidelines that apply to both objective and subjective evaluation techniques:

1. *They must be economical.* Ask yourself what is the smallest number of reports and statistics that are needed to understand and have a reasonably reliable picture of this program.

2. *They must be meaningful.* Measure significant things, never trivia.

3. *They must be appropriate.* Use criteria suitable for volunteer programs, not salesmen, recreation workers, or directors.

4. *They must be timely.* Recognize which things need rapid reporting back and which do not.

5. *They must be simple.* They must be so clear and simply stated they do not confuse people and keep them from participating. They should also be as concise as possible.

6. *They must be operational.* Action, rather than information, is the goal. Administration must have the commitment to *act on the results* or it is wasted effort and people will resent it.

SUMMARY

It's important to remember that effective volunteer programs don't just happen. They are carefully planned and managed. The essential ingredients of a successful volunteer program are:

1. A belief on the part of agency administration and staff members that volunteers are both needed and wanted in their organization.

2. A qualified paid director of volunteers to oversee the planning, implementation, and evaluation of the volunteer program.

3. An understanding of the rapidly changing realities of volunteerism—changes in the makeup of the volunteer work force, and so on.

4. A commitment of needed funds to operate an effective office of volunteers.

5. An attitude of acceptance of volunteers as unpaid staff members.

6. Proper management and supervision of the volunteers.

7. The acceptance of volunteers as valuable and accountable team members who can enrich and extend the services of paid staff members.

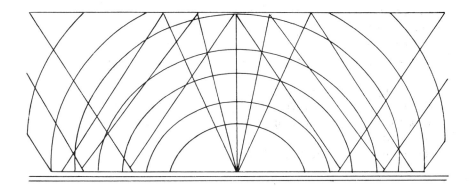

THE ROLE OF GOVERNING BOARDS IN COMMUNITY-SERVICE AGENCIES

Beverly Clifton

CHAPTER 9

"I feel a tremendous dedication to the concept of community boards for small social-service agencies. The energy consumption is great, the problems monumental, and the rewards few for those who choose this form of community involvement. The future of small community-based social-service agencies is, I believe, directly linked to the quality and effectiveness of their governing boards."

Beverly Clifton is a school nurse and health counselor in an alternative high school. She has served as a consultant to several community boards and has maintained an active membership in them. Although she enjoys her participation in the grassroots political process, her greatest satisfaction is derived from the involvement and personal friendship she has had with her students.

We will consider the following questions in this chapter:

What is the philosophy underlying the creation of governing boards for
    community-service programs?
How can a community be represented by a governing board?
How does the role of governing boards differ from that of advisory boards?
What are the criteria for membership on a governing board?

THE PHILOSOPHY UNDERLYING THE CREATION OF GOVERNING BOARDS

Grassroots input into government policies, public agencies, and cummunity programs has been given lip service for years. With the advent of community boards of directors in the late 1950s and early 1960s, such input has become a real possibility. The people who live and work in a community—people who have firsthand knowledge and strong feelings about that community—are being given a critical voice through membership on governing boards in community-service programs. In the nonprofit sector of community services, agency survival is often dependent on an active and informed governing board.

The philosophy underlying the creation of community boards of directors is based on the premise that the individuals who reside and work in a community have specialized knowledge, insights, and feelings regarding the needs of that community. Although this assumption might be correct, it might also be misleading. In order to make a meaningful contribution on a governing board, individuals need to make a real commitment of time and energy and maintain an honest belief in their community as well as in the agency they are asked to serve. Since board members are generally unpaid staff members, rewards must be derived from seeing the exciting and positive results of an agency's efforts within a community. Moreover, those who have never functioned as board members need to acquire fundamental skills in order to help guide a community-service program or agency.

There is no secret path to building a successful board or becoming an effective board member. Attitude is as important as knowledge in this regard.

COMMUNITY REPRESENTATION

Ideally, the composition and characteristics of a community board should be as varied as the community it represents. The following guidelines should suggest ways in which adequate community representation can be ensured on a board of directors:

1. The geographical area that the board represents should be clearly defined. This area may comprise an entire town or a portion of a large city. The area should then be studied. Economic groupings, political parties, racial and ethnic characteristics, and other elements that may determine the representative segments of the community should be examined.
2. The following age groups should be represented: under 21, 21 through 41, 41 through 59, and 60 and over.
3. Males and females should be equally represented on the board.
4. Representation of ethnic and racial minorities should reflect the composition of the population in the area served.
5. The board should reflect the socioeconomic status of the community.
6. There is always a need for board members who have expertise in the areas of finance and management.
7. Whenever possible, individuals who have a working knowledge of the services provided by an agency (such as job training, education, mental-health care, and so on) should be included on its board of directors.

THE ROLE OF THE GOVERNING BOARD OF DIRECTORS

The role of a governing board of directors is extensive. Its members are legally responsible for developing administrative policy regarding personnel, accounting, budgeting, community participation, financing, and the establishment of program priorities. They also help to evaluate the programs and services provided by the agency they govern. In other words, the board of directors establishes a policy and the agency implements and executes that policy.

Specifically, the board identifies needs, establishes long-term and short-term goals, formulates plans, develops policies, determines fiscal and personnel policies, approves proposals for financing programs, and ensures compliance with the stipulations of funding sources.

The specific responsibilities and authority of the governing board varies from agency to agency. Some act as advisory boards, while others act in a managerial capacity. The capacity in which a board functions is determined by the needs of the agency and the community.

The role and function of a governing board in terms of program management is limited to hiring and firing the executive director. Board members should support an executive director who is doing a creditable job. By taking a weak stance in the support of the director, the board can undermine and stifle his or her effectiveness as an administrator. The governing board should design an evaluative tool to use in assessing the performance of the executive director.

This assessment should include an evaluation of the director's ability to implement policy and reach goals and objectives established by the board.

Staff members should have access to the governing board through the organizational chain of command (with the executive director as the final spokesperson). Board members, in turn, do not have the authority to give orders or instructions directly to staff members; they must communicate with them through the executive director.

The chairperson of any governing board has an exceedingly important role: in setting the tone of the board, he or she can either inhibit progress or serve to implement change. A high degree of trust and a positive rapport between the chairperson and the executive director is an obvious asset. Open communication between the two is needed to keep the board well informed.

PLANNING POLICY

A board of directors exists primarily to plan the policies of the agency it governs. The members of a board must be familiar with current policies and determine the need for new ones. In his *Manual on Governance and Policy Planning for CMHC Boards Members,* Wolfgang Price (1975) discusses the major steps involved in planning policy. The first step entails identifying the issues. Input should come from staff, board, and community. Next, an issue-discussion paper and an issue-action paper should be prepared.

Issue-action papers deal with specific situations and policies that are narrow in scope. This type of report is usually presented at regular board meetings. Issue-discussion papers deal with general situations and policies that are broad in scope. This type of report is usually considered during informal meetings and workshops. Both issue-action papers and issue-discussion papers should include the following:

1. A statement of a problem.
2. A statement of an issue.
3. An explanation of why the problem requires board action.
4. A list of current relevant policies.
5. Possible alternatives.
6. The implications of the stated alternatives.
7. The possible consequences of inaction.

The statement of a problem should be succinct, and it should deal with situations, *not* people. A statement of issues is included only when the problem is multifaceted and cannot be clarified in a simple statement. An issue should be stated as a question or a series of questions. The question or questions should be brief and should relate directly to the statement of the problem. For example, the problem might be that a majority of staff members are not getting to work on time. In this case, the issue could include such questions as: Does the work-day begin too early? Could the schedule be modified to accomodate those who prefer to get up later? What is the daily work load?

The explanation of why board action is necessary is designed to help eliminate those issues that should be handled by administrative personnel. For example, the problem cited in the preceding paragraph is a managerial problem and should be handled by an administrative officer.

The list of current relevant policies should include policies approved by the board as well as those implicit policies that have been initiated by staff members but not formalized by board action.

The possible alternatives should include all feasible and appropriate means of dealing with a particular issue. The implications of those alternatives should be examined in depth. There may be situations in which inaction is desirable; however, if a board continually defers or fails to act on policy, it will ultimately lose credibility.

A disposition of action should be noted on an issue-action paper. A statement of disposition should specify if a policy was approved, an action was deferred, or further study was needed by the board or the staff members.

Some of the specific areas in which governing boards can initiate policy are:

1. Bylaws of the organization.
2. Personnel policies (such as salary scales, fringe benefits, job descriptions, and job specifications).
3. Administrative policies.
4. Budget and finance (such as fund raising and planning for funds after grants diminish or terminate).
5. Program priorities.
6. Program goals and objectives.
7. Board goals and objectives.
8. Needs assessment.
9. Research and evaluation (write an annual report, review the results of programs, and adjust the programs).
10. Communication with members of the community through public relations and educational programs.
11. The general operation of the organization.
12. Coordination of services.
13. Evaluation of the executive director.

LEGAL RESPONSIBILITIES OF GOVERNING BOARDS

At the Colorado State Mental Health Conference in September of 1976, Joseph de Raismus, Assistant State Attorney General, talked about the legal responsibiliteis of governing boards. He stated that "The functions and responsibilities of boards rest in what they are ultimately held accountable for in law and by the community at large." Governing boards should supervise and monitor agency programs and maintain an ongoing evaluation process that will assure continued implementation of policies as they have been prescribed. According to de Raismus, job descriptions and hiring procedures should be carefully scrutinized by board members.

A governing board is held responsible for its agency's programs and for the services or treatment that agency provides. A board can be sued if the agency it governs fails to provide proper and adequate services or treatment. As a result, board members frequently select attorneys as members so they can provide legal advice. However, boards would best be served by hiring an outside attorney for their legal counsel.

In the area of budgeting, a governing board should form an audit committee to study and formulate fiscal policy, monitor programs, and assure accountability of public funds.

DEALING WITH THE REALITIES

Often board members are actively involved in a number of activities. This involvement gives them a broader perspective and provides them with skills and information that help them to become productive board members. On the other hand, because of their involvement in various activities, they may have little time or energy to commit to the board itself. To be effective, a board member needs to attend meetings regularly and become actively involved in committees. All of this requires a significant amount of time.

Agencies should develop orientation programs or manuals for all new board members. New members need information concerning the agency and the responsibilities of the board. A well planned and executed workshop can be very valuable to the new board members as well as the "old-timers." The increasing complexity of today's social-service agencies makes it imperative that board members be kept informed of new developments in their agencies and the services they provide.

SUMMARY

The governing boards of social-service agencies are responsible for developing administrative policy regarding personnel, accounting, budgeting, community participation, financing, and the establishment of program priorities. They also help to evaluate the programs and services provided by the agency they govern.

There is no secret path to building a successful board or becoming an effective board member. Attitude is as important as knowledge in this regard.

In the nonprofit sector of community services, an agency's survival depends on an active and informed governing board.

SUGGESTED REFERENCES

Characteristics of community-wide citizen involvement programs. U.S. Government Printing Office, 1976. This publication describes various citizen-involvement programs, presents different approaches to citizen involvement, and lists some common characteristics of programs now underway.

Agency boardmanship. Cleveland, Ohio: The Federation of Catholic Community Services. This is a manual of practices and procedures for the governing boards of the agencies of Catholic Charities of Cleveland. It includes sample bylaws, model minutes, a rating scale for boards, and principles for managing a nonprofit organization.

Mathiasen, K. *Confessions of a board member.* Washington, D. C.: The Alban Institute, 1976. In this book, a management consultant to nonprofit organizations describes the life cycle of a governing board.

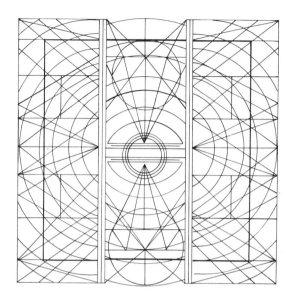

THE INTERNAL
AND EXTERNAL
POLITICS OF
AGENCY
SURVIVAL

PART FOUR

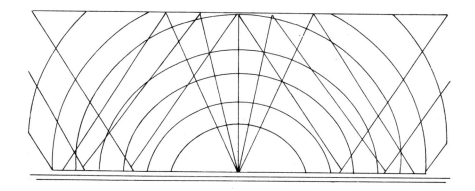

THE LOBBYING PROCESS AND THE COMMUNITY-SERVICE AGENCY

Charles McLean

CHAPTER 10

"The survival of the entire social-service system is, in my opinion, dependent on the survival of the small community-based service agency. It is no longer a question of whether or not the federal government can solve our social ills. It can't! Real solutions will come when government becomes a supportive facilitator and small community-based agencies become active implementors."

Charles McLean is the president and publisher of *a public affair,* a magazine that promotes cooperation between the private and the public sectors in solving social problems. He is also the producer of *High Time,* a 30-minute radio program that deals with problems and issues of concern to the elderly.

We will consider the following questions in this chapter:

What is a lobbyist?
What are the legal restrictions governing lobbying efforts?
What can you do to make your agency's lobbying effort more effective?

In any small community-based, social-service organization, political activity is an important consideration. The administrator of a small agency or program needs to be able to organize individuals with varied backgrounds and channel their energies toward a single goal. The motivations for individual participation are complex and are often at odds with an agency's goals. The director and staff members of social-service agencies need to identify and confront political pressures, assess those pressures, and then use them to guide their agency.

Two types of political pressure—internal and external—affect social-service agencies. Internal political pressures, which arise from within the structure of an agency, affect the operation of the staff. These are the pressures that can divide or solidify staff members. Internal politics affects the way in which staff members relate to one another and to their organization. The factors affecting the politics within an agency relate to conflict resolution (see Chapter 11).

External political pressures—the politics of the outside world—also affect social-service agencies. The media, the public, the government, and other social-service organizations are the sources of external political pressures.

The material in this chapter focuses on lobbying efforts and the social-service agency's relationship to the legislative process. We will deal with the ways in which agencies can build political relationships with legislative bodies of government and achieve their goals through the use of legislation.

WHAT IS A LOBBYIST?

Very simply, a lobbyist is a person who attempts to influence the outcome of legislation. Lobbyists are often referred to as the "third house of government." Unfortunately, many people tend to view the lobbying process as a sinister act of influence buying or pressuring. Since public attention is focused on the misconduct of some lobbyists when it does occur, the image of "backroom deals" and the illicit exchange of money is often associated with all lobbyists. Indeed, there are legislators who can be "bought," and there are lobbyists who are more than willing to buy them; however, your lobbying efforts *cannot* be based on the assumption that you can buy a legislator's vote. In reality, the most effective lobbyist is the one who can provide legislators with the most accurate information on a given issue.

KNOW THE TAX RULES

Before you begin a concentrated lobbying effort, you should become familiar with tax rules. In the U.S., nonprofit agencies may fall into any one of several tax classifications, but most charitable agencies are governed by the rules of Internal Revenue code section 501 (c) (3). Contributions made to agencies in this category are tax deductible, and the agencies pay no federal income tax.

An agency may lose its tax-exempt status if, as a substantial part of its activities, it attempts to influence legislation. Although there are no specific guidelines to help you determine just how much lobbying constitutes a substantial part of your agency's overall activities, there is case law on the subject (cases in which an organization's tax status has been challenged in court for alleged noncompliance with government regulations).

How, then, can a nonprofit agency be sure that it is complying with the law? Unfortunately, it cannot! The IRS has published a booklet that explains how to obtain and keep tax-exempt status, but the regulations are like the ice on an early winter pond. (You can read about its predicted thickness, and others can offer opinions as to its thickness, but once you've fallen through the ice, no one can correct your mistake.)

It should be noted here that the Internal Revenue Service encourages all organizations to call their local IRS offices for information and assistance.

If lobbying is to be an ongoing function of your agency, you should establish a lobbying structure before you begin. If, on the other hand, your agency intends to become involved in lobbying on a one-time basis, there is no need for the creation of a separate legal lobbying arm; however, your agency should be careful to spend none of its operating budget on the lobbying effort.

Direct contact with legislators should be made through unpaid "friends" of your agency—board members or other volunteers, who are neither paid nor reimbursed for expenses incurred in the lobbying effort.

A nonprofit agency shouldn't use its newsletters or mailing permits to influence legislation or endorse political candidates. This doesn't mean that the members of such an agency are barred from discussing legislative matters. The study, research, and discussion of matters that pertain to the government and to specific legislation may, in certain instances, be considered educational activity rather than a lobbying effort.

After considering the legalities and possible consequences of your proposed lobbying effort in light of federal regulations, your agency needs to look at state regulations. Some states have enacted "Sunshine Acts"—laws that require disclosure of funds spent on political activity. Your agency should become familiar with these regulations.

PREPARING YOUR LOBBYING EFFORT

Lobbying for your agency is a demanding job that requires a blend of knowledge, alertness, patience, and perseverance. In preparing your lobbying effort, you should investigate pertinent government regulations, become familiar with legislative procedures and reports, and study the issue(s) and bill(s) for which you plan to lobby. These steps are discussed in the following paragraphs.

Investigate Pertinent Government Regulations. Be sure your organization is in complicance with all state and federal regulations. Study your state's registration requirements, disclosure laws, and any other regulations that apply to lobbyists.

Become Familiar With Legislative Procedures and Reports. Sit in the galleries of the house and senate during their sessions. Attend legislative committee meetings. Visit the bill room to obtain information such as: updated copies of bills, status sheets on bills, a subject index of all bills, house and senate calendars, schedules of floor business and committee meetings, and house and senate journals.

Most state legislatures print booklets or handouts of the legislative districts in the state, information concerning the lawmakers, and so on. This kind of information will help you to organize your lobby effort.

Study the Issue(s) and Bill(s) for Which You Plan to Lobby. Know the facts. Knowledge is important to your credibility. Because legislators are concerned with hundreds of bills, they rely a great deal on lobbyists to furnish them with accurate information on which to base their decisions. You and the members of the organization you represent need to study the issue(s) and bill(s) for which you plan to lobby. Some of the resources you can use are:

1. Newspaper articles that deal with your issue or with the legislators.
2. The legislative research office. Most legislatures have some type of research arm. By using the information available from this source, you can find out if studies have been made on your issue.
3. State agencies that have data and information related to your issue.

ESTABLISHING YOUR AGENCY'S "PRESENCE"

The agency that is always represented by well informed individuals gains respect and credibility in the eyes of lobbyists as well as lawmakers. In order to establish your agency's presence, you'll need to wait for committee hearings and floor action on your bill and choose the appropriate moment to talk to legislators. Make this a productive time. Watch and listen. Count votes. Observe who is talking to whom. Mingle with others who are watching the legislative process. Talk to the "veteran" lobbyists. Observe the manner and style of various legislators.

APPROACHING A LEGISLATOR

You can open a conversation with a legislator simply by saying "Senator _____," or "Representative _____, may I have a word with you?" Identify yourself and the group you represent, state the name and number of the bill you are concerned with, and describe the bill briefly to refresh the legislator's memory. (The legislator may be a sponsor who hasn't had an opportunity to study the bill. In this case, you can be very helpful with your background information.) Use facts, figures, and examples to support your remarks.

You might want to provide the legislators with some printed information or an amendment to your bill. Remember that legislators' time is valuable. Your material should be concise and, above all, *accurate.*

Where and when can you talk to legislators? You might have an opportunity to talk with them in the lobby or hall before or after a committee meeting. If you need to speak with a legislator during session, hand a note to the sergeant at arms at the chamber door. If the legislator is able to talk with you, he or she will either come out to see you or, if chamber rules permit, invite you to come inside.

TESTIFYING IN COMMITTEE

You can arrange to speak in a committee meeting by signing up with the committee's assigned staff person before the meeting starts. Testimony given in committee hearings is a major source of knowledge for legislators. Your lobbying effort can be most effective in these meetings.

When you speak at a committee meeting, be prepared. You can either read a statement or speak informally. If you think it will help your presentation, you can include a chart or an illustration. Whenever you use visuals, however, be sure that they're well done and that the information on them can be easily understood. Simplicity, brevity, and clarity should be your criteria when you testify in committee.

The committee members may ask you questions after you've testified. When you answer their questions, remember that they will respect intellectual honesty, knowledge, accuracy, and an ability to focus clearly on the issue in question. (Note: If you want to propose an amendment to a bill, a committee member or the bill's sponsor(s) should be advised of this before the meeting begins.)

If you are unable to tesitfy before a particular committee, contact each committee member in person or by letter. When you write to committee members, list the name and number of the bill you're writing about and state your case briefly and accurately. Be factual, not emotional. If friends, staff members, or clients of your agency want to write, don't use form letters.

STATEHOUSE ETIQUETTE

Lobbying is an absorbing exercise in human relations. When you represent your agency, observe the conventions of behavior that are a part of the statehouse atmosphere. Never lie to a legislator, a committee member, or another lobbyist. Don't stretch the truth, and don't offer opinions on matters of which you aren't informed. Maintain a sense of humor; don't be afraid to laugh, particularly at yourself. Humor can relieve a great deal of pressure in a stressful situation. Lawmakers hear a number of complaints. Let them hear you say "thank you" for the help they provided in committee or on the floor, for supporting your bill, or for sharing their time with you.

LOBBYING: A YEAR-ROUND JOB

Your lobbying efforts should begin before the legislature convenes. Between sessions, most state legislatures hold interim committee meetings to discuss special topics. During the interim season, you can prepare legislation that you would like to see passed in the next session, meet with legislators, and line up lobbying coalitions. It isn't necessary for you to actually write a bill, but you do need a state representative or a state senator to sponsor and introduce your bill. Each state legislature has a staff of attorneys who write bills and amendments.

SUMMARY

This chapter has concentrated on the lobbying process at the state legislative level; however, the steps and principles described here can be applied to the local level as well. City councils are frequently ignored by social-service agencies, yet they represent an important branch of government. In some cities, the city council controls large amounts of federal funds. Your agency should research the city council in your area to determine its power as a potential funding source.

State agencies are also important to the attainment of a social-service organization's goals. These agencies should be researched thoroughly by a member of your organization. A large part of the lobbying battle is initial research—determining which segments of government can be used to advance your agency's goals.

There is nothing sinister about lobbying for your agency. Effective lobbying requires honesty, research, and accuracy.

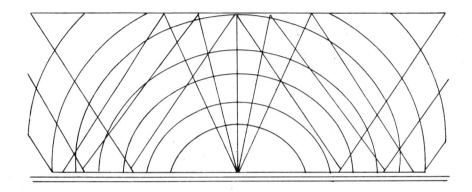

CONFLICT RESOLUTION: A PROBLEM-SOLVING APPROACH FOR COMMUNITY-SERVICE AGENCIES

John Nicoletti
Lottie Benz

CHAPTER 11

"Conflict resolution is an essential part of the politics of survival for small community-based, social-service agencies. Conflict stems from differences in values. In order to understand conflict, we need to understand fear, power, freedom, authority, and justice."

John Nicoletti and Lottie Benz are consulting psychologists and former community-health directors. They bring both a professional and a practical background of experience to the problems and conflicts confronting small community-based, social-service agencies. Although they both teach on a part-time basis, their active involvement with local grassroots organizations brings them the greatest amount of satisfaction.

We will consider the following questions in this chapter:

What is conflict?
Can conflict be beneficial?
How can you develop a system for the resolution of conflicts?
How can the effects of conflict resolution be measured?
When should you develop a conflict-resolution model?

WHAT IS CONFLICT?

Conflict is a broad-based term that is used to describe many different situations and problems. Anyone who has worked with small community-based, social-service agencies has seen conflict stem from differences over program development, fund raising, volunteer recruitment, goal setting, and so on. Listing examples of conflict can be an endless activity. Suffice it to say that conflict resolution is a task that we are faced with daily in our work as well as in our private lives. Most of our difficulties can be traced to the way in which we deal with these conflicts. Staff members and directors of social-service agencies must remember that conflict can be a strong positive force. Walton (1969) lists five specific benefits that can be derived from a conflict situation:

1. It can increase motivation and energy required to do tasks.
2. It can increase innovativeness of individuals and the system because of the diversity of views along with heightening a sense of necessity.
3. It can increase in each person an understanding of his or her own position, because the individual is forced to articulate his or her views and bring forth supporting arguments.
4. It can provide greater awareness of the individual's own identity.
5. It can be a means of managing the participant's own internal conflicts [p. 24].

In order to deal effectively with most conflicts, it's necessary to develop a model, or a systematic mechanism, for resolving problems and conflicts prior to their occurrence. The negative aspects of conflict become apparent when problems are dealt with in a "reactive" way in the middle of a crisis. The development of a systematic model for resolving conflicts is especially critical when conflicts affect the workings of an agency or an organization, because the factors that influence conflict at this level are numerous and complex.

The material in this chapter focuses on the techniques of conflict resolution employed by social-service agencies. The model we are suggesting to resolve conflicts within a system involves seven interrelated stages:

1. Assessing the system.
2. Identifying the conflict.
3. Setting goals.
4. Generating plans of action.
5. Critiquing and prioritizing plans of action.
6. Selecting and implementing a plan of action.
7. Evaluating results and revising techniques.

Your decision to use this model should be based on the effectiveness of your agency's current approach to conflict resolution. If the system your agency is using seems to be working, there is probably no need to change it. The model outlined in this chapter should be viewed as an alternative to be used separately or in combination with other models.

ASSESSING THE SYSTEM

In this first stage, your agency needs to conduct a critical evaluation of itself. This step is often passed over because it is difficult and time consuming; however, it is essential. When you assess your agency, you take a hard and sophisticated look at its stated goals and its ability to achieve those goals. (Is it doing what it's supposed to be doing?)

At the agency level, many conflicts can, no doubt, be resolved through the application of basic common sense; however, in the long run, conflict resolution will be successful if it is based on more than intuitive insight or trial-and-error methods. At the very least, this first stage should involve a review of your agency's goals and the procedures being used to achieve them.

IDENTIFYING THE CONFLICT

Once the assessment of your agency has been completed, the identification of the conflict can begin. Conflicts within an agency stem from behaviors and actions that cause problems in communication and morale.

Most agency conflicts fall into one or more of the following categories:

1. Conflicts between the agency and the community.
2. Conflicts between the agency and its funding or controlling sources.
3. Conflicts among agencies.
4. Conflicts among management personnel.
5. Conflicts between management and staff.
6. Conflicts among staff members.
7. Personal conflicts.

These categories can help you to determine which individuals or groups should be involved or considered in the resolution of a particular conflict. When identifying conflicts, it's important to describe problems in behavioral terms. *Bad morale* is a term used to describe a set of actions; however, bad morale is also the result of certain kinds of behavior. In order to eliminate bad morale, you have to deal with the behaviors that are causing it. For example, bad morale may have something to do with people who are frequently absent or who come to work late. These are specific behaviors, and once they are defined, a means of changing or improving them can be developed.

You can determine the reasons for certain behaviors by talking with the individuals involved and by observing them. You should use both methods, since people's statements and evaluations may not reflect the entire problem. If a particular behavior, or set of actions, is related to the conflict you're trying to identify, it's helpful to determine how frequently that behavior occurs. This is not always a simple task, since it's difficult to "count and measure" certain kinds of behavior.

SETTING GOALS

After the conflict has been identified and categorized, the next stage—setting goals—is initiated. In this stage, you need to decide exactly what is to be accomplished. When setting goals, it's important to keep in mind that there should be short-term and long-term goals. Your long-term goal is to resolve the conflict totally; however, realistic and obtainable short-term goals also should be developed. A serious conflict cannot be resolved overnight.

GENERATING PLANS OF ACTION

Once your goals have been established, you need to develop plans of action—methods of achieving those goals. Typically, action plans are generated through discussion—the simple exchange of ideas and thoughts. In using this approach, individuals meet to make suggestions and discuss the merits and short-comings of those suggestions. However, when this method is used, people are required to ask for solutions and evaluate those solutions almost simultaneously. Usually, when individuals or groups try to generate solutions to problems in this manner, their meetings dissolve into arguments. Moreover, this approach can be very threatening to the parties immediately involved.

Brainstorming is a more effective method of generating plans of actions. What is important about this technique is that ideas are *generated,* but they aren't *evaluated.* Evaluation is done at a later stage. It's usually beneficial to brainstorm in large groups, because, as more people are involved, a wider range of ideas is likely to be presented. The rules of brainstorming are: (1) any idea or solution is welcome, (2) individuals are encouraged to generate as many ideas as possible, and (3) ideas are *not* evaluated during the brainstorming session.

After a problem has been presented, participants in a brainstorming session suggest whatever solutions come to mind. (As a good warm-up exercise, the group could brainstorm ways of improving men's pants. This is an enjoyable exercise that illustrates how the process works.) As ideas are presented, they should be recorded by two people. Once the process gets going and ideas come very quickly from the group, the two recorders can alternate. It's important to remember that there is no discussion or evaluation of ideas at this time—they are simply stated and recorded.

Several benefits can accrue from the use of this technique: (1) time is saved, (2) individuals don't feel as though they have to defend their ideas and suggestions, and (3) the ideas presented become the property of the group as a whole.

CRITIQUING AND PRIORITIZING PLANS OF ACTION

After brainstorming is completed, the critiquing and prioritizing stage is initiated. This is the stage in which all the brainstorming ideas are evaluated, discussed, and prioritized. First, go through the list of ideas and eliminate those that the group feels are totally inappropriate. If there is any disagreement concerning a particular idea, that idea should remain on the list. After the inappropriate suggestions have been dropped, the group can go back and evaluate the remaining ideas. They might find it helpful to list the pros and cons of each idea, and then rate each of those pros and cons on a scale of 1 (not very important) to 10 (extremely important).

After each idea has been critiqued, prioritizing begins. Solutions that can be implemented immediately are placed near the top of the list, while solutions that can't be immediately implemented (or that involve a number of tasks) are placed lower on the list.

SELECTING AND IMPLEMENTING A PLAN OF ACTION

Selection follows prioritizing. Solutions that appear near the top of the list are selected for possible implementation. It isn't necessary to choose only *one* solution. In many cases, more than one solution can be utilized in dealing with a conflict. You should make sure that the solutions are feasible and that short-term and long-term consequences have been considered.

Selection must be followed by implementation. Often agencies generate and select solutions to conflicts but never get around to actually implementing those solutions. A commitment on the part of your agency to implement a plan of action is extremely important. This commitment should be shared by management, paid staff members, volunteers, and clients. It's impossible to successfully implement a plan of action without the support of all participants.

During the implementation stage, decisions should be made that answer the following questions:

1. *Who* is going to be involved in the implementation of the action plan?
2. *What* specific actions are to be taken?
3. *Who* will be affected by the implementation of the plan?
4. *When* will the implementation begin?
5. *Where* will the implementation begin?
6. *How often* should this action plan be implemented?

In making these decisions, agency administrators assign specific responsibilities and time lines to individuals. Time lines are needed in order to prevent day-to-day activities from taking precedence over the implementation of an action plan. By assigning responsibilities and time lines, administrators can determine if an action plan is resolving a conflict. When a plan of action involves a specific activity performed by certain individuals along a time line, pinpointing a breakdown in that plan of action becomes a matter of determining at what point or with which individual(s) the plan isn't working.

EVALUATING RESULTS AND REVISING TECHNIQUES

During the final stage of conflict resolution, you need to evaluate your plan's problem-solving effectiveness, or evaluate at what point in the process a breakdown occurred. This evaluation will require a review of the total process. Ask yourself the following questions: "What are our goals? What was identified as the problem? What solutions were implemented? Have things changed?" If there has been a significant positive change, the plan is working and there is no need for revision; however, if change is nonexistent or minimal, the process must be revised.

Revision involves an analysis of each stage of the conflict-resolution model to determine at what point a breakdown occurred. (Is the plan unsuccessful because the conflict wasn't correctly identified? Were the solutions implemented incorrectly? Were inappropriate solutions selected?) In this manner, agency problems and conflicts can be evaluated in a systematic way rather than through trial and error.

SUMMARY

In this chapter, we've presented a model for resolving conflicts within community-service agencies. Emphasis was placed on the advantages of taking a systematic, *proactive* approach when dealing with conflicts.

The conflict-resolution model we presented involves seven main stages:

1. Assessing the system.
2. Identifying the conflict.
3. Setting goals.
4. Generating plans of action.
5. Critiquing and prioritizing plans of action.
6. Selecting and implementing a plan of action.
7. Evaluating results and revising techniques.

Your agency will have to make an initial investment of time and effort in developing this model, but it's a wise investment. You will save more by using the techniques of conflict resolution described here than by employing a policy of management-by-crisis.

SUGGESTED REFERENCES

Aulepp, L., & Delworth, U. *Training manual for an eco-system model.* Boulder, Co.: Western Interstate Commission for Higher Education, 1976. This manual provides a step-by-step model of the ecological approach to problem solving.

Filley, A. *Interpersonal conflict resolution.* Glenview, Ill.: Scott, Foresman Co., 1975. This book focuses on the techniques used to change conflict situations into problem-solving and constructive situations.

Walton, R. *Interpersonal peacemaking: Confrontations and third-party peacemaking.* Reading, Mass.: Addison-Wesley, 1969. Walton focuses on interpersonal conflict in organizations and the role of third-party consultants. He examines the importance of conflict and discusses some ways in which it can be viewed.

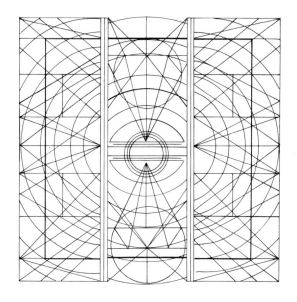

STAFF AND LEADERSHIP DEVELOPMENT

PART FIVE

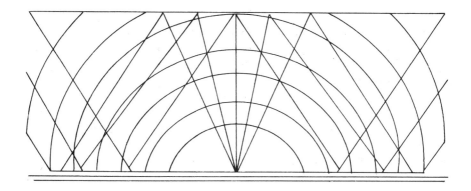

ORGANIZATIONAL INFLUENCES, INDIVIDUAL BEHAVIOR, AND STYLES OF LEADERSHIP

Kent Higgins

CHAPTER 12

"Directors, coordinators, and staff members of small community-based, social-service agencies are realizing, in increasing numbers, that it is they themselves who make their programs effective. There will always be external constraints and obstacles, but the people who make up an agency must look inward for the definition of rights, privileges, roles, and responsibilities."

Kent Higgins has had experience in public relations, media development, and professional writing. He is currently a journalism instructor. His special interests in affirmative-action programs, photography, and classical choral music take up most of his spare time.

We will consider the following questions in this chapter:

What factors influence social-service agencies?
How do individual behavior patterns affect styles of leadership?
How can you determine your own style of leadership?

The goals and objectives of small community-based, social-service agencies are affected by their members' individual behavior patterns and styles of leadership. Since these agencies range from storefront operations to subunits of government, their members assume a variety of leadership styles and behavior patterns. In order to improve the effectiveness of your own agency, you need to acquire a basic understanding of these styles and patterns.

To identify the ways in which various members of an organization influence one another, you need to: (1) understand the organization, and (2) examine individual behavioral patterns. Once you understand the organizational and personal dynamics of your agency, you can determine which style of leadership will be most effective in your situation.

INTERNAL INFLUENCES

A program or agency director can influence the people, the work structure, and the systems and rules of his or her organization. Each of these factors can be considered the side of a triangle that represents an organization. A change in size of any one of the sides will result in a change in the overall shape of the organization. In every community-service agency, changes occur constantly. For example, when a staff member is assigned to a new position (people), the change creates a new work assignment (work structure) and, therefore, a change in the information and reporting mechanisms (systems and rules) of the organization.

EXTERNAL INFLUENCES

Organizations are surrounded by influences that have a profound effect on their operations but are outside their direct control. The reassignment of a staff member affects the people, the work structure, and the rules and systems of an organization. These are all internal changes that can be seen fairly easily as they take place. However, the *reasons* for the reassignment and the *impact* on the people who make up the organization are not as easily identified. The reasons and the impact are affected by external influences; they come about as a result of the organization's existence in a total environment. In your home, for example, a fairly clear, *internal* decision might be made to determine who is going to mow the lawn and who is going to wash the clothes. However, the basis on which that decision is made has a great deal to do with sex roles (culture), the automatic washer and the power lawnmower (technology), and the purpose of a family or marriage (goals).

The three principal external influences that affect an agency are: culture, goals, and technology. Each of these, along with the three internal influences mentioned earlier, affects the operation of social-service agencies. An overview of these internal and external influences is illustrated in Figure 12-1.

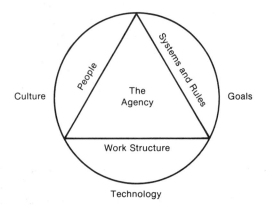

FIGURE 12-1. Influences Affecting Social-Service Agencies.

CULTURES

The culture enveloping an agency includes a set of deep-seated beliefs concerning the way in which people should work, the way in which they should be managed, and so on. Obviously, the cultural environment of a community-action center is quite different from that of a Wall Street brokerage firm. Charles B. Handy (1976) has divided agencies into four categories: (1) power oriented, (2) role oriented, (3) task oriented, and (4) people oriented. Let us now examine each of these categories.

Power-Oriented Agencies. Agencies in this category look inward to a hub—the central power source. Power is held either by a select number of key individuals or by one person; therefore, the organization's success or failure is determined by the central power source. The typical director of a power-oriented agency is action-oriented and politically minded. He or she is very willing to take risks in an effort to increase the possibilities of the agency's success.

Role-Oriented Agencies. Role-oriented agencies emphasize role relationships. The members of this type of agency work under the principles of logic, rationality, and caution. The agency itself could be represented by a triangle supported by a number of vertical legs. The strength of the unit depends on the legs holding up the triangle. For example, the legs might represent the departments of a large agency (such as finance, accounting, training, personnel, and so on). The roles of the individual members of such an agency are clearly defined in policies and memoranda.

Role-oriented agencies often frustrate power-oriented individuals, who desire control over their work. The focus of these agencies is on the organization rather than the individuals who make up the organization. Size often has a great deal to do with whether an agency is influenced by roles; however, this influence can be seen even in small agencies.

Task-Oriented Agencies. The third type of agency is task-oriented, or project-oriented. The emphasis here is to get a job done by bringing together the appropriate resources and people. The team concept makes this type of agency very adaptive. Groups are formed for specific purposes.

There is no typical manager or administrator of a task-oriented agency. Group members have a high degree of control over their own work. Each member has respect for the other team members—respect that is based on expertise rather than status—and they judge one another's performance by team results.

People-Oriented Agencies. This type of agency could be described as a set of single-cell organisms living in the same solution but remaining independent of one another. Commonly, such an agency consists of a group of people who have banded together to enhance their individual self-interests. The extent to which resources and facilities are shared depends on the needs of each individual member. There is no typical manager or administrator of this type of agency; each individual is "the central point."

GOALS

The goals of an agency are influenced by a variety of factors: staff and budget support, availability of resources, external demands for services, and so on. Administrators of social-service agencies need to ask themselves the following question: "Does our agency have a set of goals that is *accepted* and *strived* for by our members, or are our goals simply vague pledges made to satisfy funding requirements and special-interest groups?"

TECHNOLOGY

Technology is the last environmental factor to be dealt with in describing the influences that affect the operation of community-service agencies. Technology, if properly adapted, can enhance the efficiency of small agencies, but it can also produce a negative psychological impact. For example, there is a trend now among small agencies to form a consortium in order to pay for and utilize the services of a computer. The fact is that computers are faster, less susceptible to error, and more dependable than people. But staff members who are affected by such an arrangement may feel they have been replaced by an impersonal machine.

The incorporation of technology into community-service agencies is here to stay, but so are the people who make up those agencies. Administrators must consider the feelings of staff members prior to, during, and after the introduction of technological systems into their agencies.

INDIVIDUAL BEHAVIOR PATTERNS

An administrator's style of leadership has a direct effect on the balance found in any agency among people, work structures, and systems and rules. Conversely, the behavior patterns of individual staff members require specific leadership styles in order to maximize the motivation of each person. Schein (1965) identifies four basic sets of behavior that can greatly influence the type of leadership style a director or administrator of an agency might find most effective: rational-economic behavior, social individual behavior, self-actualizing behavior, and complex individual behavior.

Rational-Economic Behavior. This type of behavior is exhibited by individuals who dislike their work and avoid it whenever possible. Such individuals are basically motivated and controlled by the security of their jobs. It's understandably difficult for an administrator to deal effectively with this type of behavior. Perhaps the best approach is to transcend the behavior, in which the administrator simply assumes responsibility for the person's performance on the job.

Social Individual Behavior. Individuals who exhibit this type of behavior maintain good relationships with their coworkers. A congenial work situation is extremely important to them. If such an individual sees that organizational objectives are stressed more than personal needs, his or her psychological energy might be directed toward personal dissatisfaction, apathy, conflict, tension, or opposition to the organization's objectives.

Self-Actualizing Behavior. Individuals who have a hierarchy of needs exhibit self-actualizing behavior. As "lower-order" needs are satisfied, "higher-order" needs are acquired. Maslow (1954) ranks these needs (from lowest to highest): (1) physiological needs, (2) safety needs, (3) the need for belongingness and love, (4) the need for esteem, and (5) the need for self-actualization. It is particularly important for an administrator to be able to recognize those individuals who have reached the self-actualizing level. These individuals have much self-direction and self-control. Administrators need to be ingenious enough to tap this wealth of energy and enthusiasm.

Complex Individual Behavior. This type of behavior is exhibited by people who alter their behavior patterns frequently. These people change and develop in an organization at varying paces. The changes in their behavior patterns are often influenced by the internal and external variables that affect organizations. Administrators need the unique ability to recognize these changes and react appropriately. The staff members of today's community-based social-service organizations exhibit all the behavior patterns we've discussed here, and they vary greatly in experience, education, position, and status. It's up to the director or administrator of each agency to develop leadership qualities that will best utilize and maximize the energies and talents of individual staff members.

IDENTIFYING AND CHOOSING A STYLE OF LEADERSHIP

Robert Blake and Jean Mouton have developed a questionnaire that identifies leadership patterns. The questions deal with how one perceives decisions, convictions, conflicts, emotions, and goal achievement. Based on their responses to these questions, individuals are placed in one of five categories of managerial style. These categories are: impoverished management, task management, middle-of-the-road management, country-club management, and team management.

Impoverished Management. Neither production nor sound relationships are essential. This leader tries to remain uninvolved or neutral and see that established procedures are carried out.

Task Management. Good relationships are incidental and secondary to high production. This leader sees to it that production goals are met by planning, directing, and controlling all work.

Middle-of-the-Road Management. A balance between high production and good human relations is the aim of this person. This type of leader tries to find a middle ground in an attempt to achieve a reasonable amount of production without destroying morale.

Country-Club Management. Production is incidental, and it is secondary to good relations. This leader wants harmonious relationships and a work environment that is secure and pleasant.

Team Management. This leader attempts to encourage production by using participative involvement of staff members. Decisions are made collectively, and the administrator is, in effect, just another member of the team.

Robert Tannenbaum and Warren H. Schmidt (1958 & 1973) have identified seven styles of leadership. Each of these is identified by the specific actions a leader takes in arriving at a decision:

Low-trust level

High-trust level

1. Makes decisions and announces them.
2. "Sells" decisions to others.
3. Presents decisions and invites questions.
4. Presents tentative decisions.
5. Presents a problem, obtains suggestions, and then makes the final decision.
6. Defines limits but allows staff members to make decisions.
7. All staff members participate in the decision-making process.

SUMMARY

A program or agency director can influence the people, the work structure, and the systems and rules of his or her organization. Each of these factors is constantly changing, and to accomodate these changes, the structure or shape of the organization also must change.

The most significant external influences affecting the operation of an organization are culture, goals, and technology. All of these influences are constantly interacting with one another. The result is a continuing process of change that goes on within the agency. A director or administrator of an agency needs to examine his or her own behavior pattern as it relates to leadership. An administrator's style of leadership has a direct effect on the balance found in any agency among people, work structures, and systems and rules.

Schein identifies four basic sets of behavior that determine the leadership style of administrators: rational-economic behavior, social individual behavior, self-actualizing behavior, and complex individual behavior.

Blake and Mouton's questionnaire identifies five leadership patterns: impoverished management, task management, middle-of-the-road management, country-club management, and team management.

SUGGESTED REFERENCES

Cornuelle, R. *De-managing America: The final revolution.* New York: Bantam Books, 1977. This book presents a philosophical approach to management by the former executive director of the National Association of Manufacturers. The basic theme is that we tend to overmanage just about everything in the U.S.

Handy, C. B. *Understanding organizations.* Baltimore: Penguin Books, 1976. Handy approaches organizations on a practical level. He deals with the ways in which basic concepts can be applied effectively. His book contains workable models for practical problem solving.

Schumacher, E. F. *Small is beautiful.* New York: Perennial Library, 1973. The subtitle of Schumacher's book is "Economics as if People Mattered." It should be considered "must reading" for the director of any small community-service agency.

Steele, F., & Jenks, S. *The feel of the work place.* Reading, Mass.: Addison-Wesley, 1977. In this book, the authors compare changes in work environments to changes in the weather. There are "stormy" days (days filled with problems and crises) in every agency. The authors provide valuable insight into effective administration on such days.

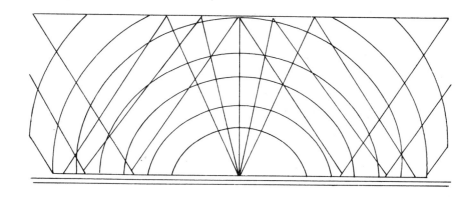

EMOTIONAL
SURVIVAL

Alan Dahms

CHAPTER 13

"Grassroots administration requires a special talent. Attempting to do the seemingly impossible with limited resources tests our creative abilities as well as our emotional and physical stamina. I believe each of us tends to overlook our own needs."

Alan Dahms is fascinated by the dynamics of healthful functioning, the elements of stress management, and the psychology of the helping relationship. His activities include jogging, teaching, consulting, and flying a small plane.

We will consider the following questions in this chapter:

What are thriving skills?
Why is it important to use choosing skills?
What is personal-cost accounting?
Why is it dangerous to accept "alleged" limitations?

INTRODUCTION

The material in this chapter is designed to influence behavior. If you accept my invitation to focus more attention on your own needs, an important process will be set in motion. You will come to perceive your own choices, costs, risks, and life-style options in new ways. The need for action on your part will seem more immediate.

The preceding chapters in this book dealt with programs, communications, volunteer support systems, agency survival, and leadership styles; this chapter focuses on emotional survival from *your* point of view.

I have discovered more questions than answers while writing this chapter:

Why do we ignore the emotional needs in ourselves and others?
Why do we sometimes behave so ineffectively?
Why do we sacrifice the precious present moment on the altars of *past* and
   future?
Why do we tend to put *things* ahead of *persons?*

I am often amazed by the way in which administrators of social-service agencies react when I ask them what they're doing to take care of themselves. Many of them answer by saying "I've never thought of that. After all, I'm here to help others. I've completed academic work in human services, social work, community services, and business, and no one *ever* invited me to put myself first. I was taught how to help others." As you work through this chapter, which could have been subtitled *How to Get from Here to There Intact,* I want to ask you to think about *your* needs. If you ignore those needs, you will pay an exorbitant personal and professional price.

Administrators of small social-service agencies deal with conflicts between staff members and volunteers, self-serving board members, part-time clerical help, piles of urgent phone messages, negative publicity, and on and on. How do they survive emotionally? What skills do they need? During the past several years, I've asked administrators these questions to determine why some are victims of stress, whereas others seem to use stressful situations to further their own growth.

THRIVING SKILLS

By analyzing hundreds of responses from individuals regarding their methods of surviving emotionally, I've been able to identify four thriving skills (Dahms, 1980): (1) the ability to maximize available choices, (2) the ability to monitor personal costs and benefits in all situations, (3) the ability to challenge alleged limitations by taking risks, and (4) the ability to assume responsibility for designing a unique lifestyle.

These skills are examined in the following sections.

Each of needs to practice these skills every day. What we know is of no help to us unless we apply it. I want to invite you to consider how important these skills are as you meet, or choose *not* to meet, your day-to-day responsibilities. I encourage you to answer the questions included in this chapter and examine the list of suggested references at the end of the chapter.

THE ABILITY TO MAXIMIZE AVAILABLE CHOICES

Thrivers believe that it's better to make choices than to default by refusing to act. They realize that choosing involves taking risks and they assume responsibility for the consequences of their choices. They know that one excellent definition of *emotional illness* is "the inability to perceive available choices." They recognize the dangers inherent in waiting for others to initiate change; they initiate needed changes on their own. For example, you can choose your occupation. If you feel trapped at present, you need to consider some alternatives. You *do* have a choice. By 1985, an estimated 75% of the labor force in the U.S. will be producing services or goods that aren't yet available. The average person today can expect to experience five to seven major career changes in his or her lifetime. Effective choosing skills have never been more important.

The process of choosing includes *selecting* certain beliefs that are personally valued and then *acting* in terms of those beliefs and values. Choosing skills are most effective when individuals have a clear understanding of their own belief/value systems. A number of exercises that are useful in exploring value systems can be found in *Values Clarification* (Simon, Howe, & Kirschenbaum, 1972).

Individuals who neglect to develop their choosing skills may become victims of their own version of the South Indian monkey trap. The trap consists of a hollowed-out coconut chained to a stake. The coconut contains rice that can be grabbed through a small hole. The hole is big enough to accommodate a monkey's hand but not a fist filled with rice. When a monkey reaches into the coconut, it becomes trapped; it doesn't "choose" to release the rice. You need to remember that you have choices, and you need to learn how to develop choosing skills.

Choosing Relationships. The most critical choices individuals have to make are those that determine with whom they relate. Although these choices are important to everyone, they are particularly important to those individuals who provide human services. On what do people base these choices? Each of us learns at an early age that many people are different from ourselves; in fact, more people are different than are similar. We are made aware of the fact that others do not share our family name, economic status, skin color, or physical health.

Since we learn to categorize individuals so early in life, several groups within the human family—older persons, for instance—gain automatic low status. To be effective, social-service administrators need to unlearn these categories and rediscover the needs shared by *all* members of the human family.

Our society makes it easy for us to harm those who look and act differently from ourselves. Children are often taught by well meaning parents, and later by society in general, that certain people are "different." They often learn to use words such as *gook, jap, commie, queer, spic, hippie, gimp, nigger,* and so on. Unfortunately, little people who learn prejudice become big people who view Blacks, Anglos, Native Americans, Mexican Americans, senior citizens, gays, handicapped persons, and others as different—so different that inflicting injury on them (psychological or physical) is not considered wrong. As children then, many people learn to base their actions on what Slater (1970) calls the *toilet assumption*—that is, the notion that unwanted matter (unwanted difficulties) will disappear if it is removed from our immediate field of vision. Those who base their attitudes and behavior on this assumption deal with social problems by decreasing their visibility. Examples of this approach abound in our society: the flight to the suburbs, the isolation of the ghettos, the institutionalization of the aged and the physically and emotionally handicapped, and so on. As a result, the underlying problems of our society are removed from daily experience and consciousness, and the knowledge, skills, and motivation needed to deal with them are lacking.

List some categories of people that exist from your personal point of view, the source of your attitude toward these people, and the ways in which your behavior toward them reveals your feelings about them.

PERSONAL-COST ACCOUNTING

You can't help others if you aren't good to yourself. By becoming a victim of a choice-blind monkey trap, you engage in behaviors that exact enormous personal costs. For example you might ignore messages from your internal "personal-cost accountant" that indicate you are overtired and overextended. You might associate with people who drain your energies and cause you to feel depressed (the death dealers), and fail to relate to people who give you energy and extend growth invitations to you (the life givers). You might refuse to give yourself permission to be good to yourself.

Depression (the "common cold" of emotional problems), feelings of helplessness or hopelessness, insomnia, and loss of appetite signify that personal costs exceed personal benefits. By adopting a stiff-upper-lip attitude and disregarding your own well-being, you invite high blood pressure, heart attack, bleeding ulcers, ulcerative colitis, and emotional turmoil.

Life-Change Stress. Major changes and developments over which individuals have little control are sources of a great amount of stress. Recent research shows that a relationship exists between stress and illness and that, in many instances, reaction to stress precipitates physical as well as emotional illness.

Thomas H. Holmes (1967), a psychiatrist at the University of Washington, has devised a system to simplify the prediction and recognition of stress-related illnesses. Holmes and his colleagues at the University of Washington School of Medicine constructed the following scale of stress values measured in "life-change units" (LCUs). They predict that those who score more than 300 LCU points on this scale are more likely to develop a major illness within the next two years than those who score less than 300.

Check the life-change events that you've experienced during the past two years and add the points for your LCU total. (Include the number of times you've experienced each of the events listed.)

THE SOCIAL READJUSTMENT RATING SCALE[1]

Rank	Life Event	Mean Value
1.	Death of a spouse	___100
2.	Divorce	___ 73
3.	Marital separation	___ 65
4.	Jail term (over one week)	___ 63
5.	Death of a close family member	___ 63
6.	Major personal injury or serious illness	___ 53
7.	Marriage	___ 50
8.	Fired from work	___ 47
9.	Marital reconciliation	___ 45
10.	Retirement	___ 45
11.	Major change in health of a family member	___ 44
12.	Pregnancy	___ 40
13.	Sexual difficulties	___ 39

[1] Adapted from "The Social Readjustment Rating Scale," by T. H. Holmes and R. H. Rahe, *Journal of Psychosomatic Research*, 1967, 11, 213-218. Copyright 1967 by Pergamon Press, Limited. Reprinted by permission.

Rank	Life Event	Mean Value
14.	Addition of a family member	__ 39
15.	Business readjustment	__ 39
16.	Change in financial status	__ 38
17.	Death of a close friend	__ 37
18.	Change to a different line of work	__ 36
19.	Increase in the number of arguments with spouse	__ 35
20.	Mortgage over $10,000	__ 31
21.	Foreclosure of mortgage or loan	__ 30
22.	Change in responsibilities at work	__ 29
23.	Son or daughter leaving home	__ 29
24.	Trouble with in-laws	__ 29
25.	Outstanding personal achievement	__ 28
26.	Husband or wife finds or leaves a job	__ 26
27.	Start or finish school	__ 26
28.	Change in living conditions	__ 25
29.	Revision of personal habits	__ 24
30.	Trouble with boss	__ 23
31.	Change in work hours or conditions	__ 20
32.	Change in residence	__ 20
33.	Change in schools	__ 20
34.	Change in recreation activities	__ 19
35.	Change in church activities	__ 19
36.	Change in social activities	__ 18
37.	Mortgage or loan less than $10,000	__ 17
38.	Change in sleeping habits	__ 16
39.	Change in the number of family get-togethers	__ 15
40.	Change in eating habits	__ 15
41.	Vacation	__ 13
42.	Christmas	__ 12
43.	Minor violation of the law	__ 11
	Total LCU	__

Holmes and his associates have retested this scale with thousands of subjects in several different countries. The probability is that about 90% of those who have more than 450 LCUs will become ill in the near future. It's important to note, however, that this cause-and-effect relationship between stress and illness isn't absolute. I've filled out the scale twice within the past four years, and each time my LCU total exceeded 400. (I haven't yet become ill!)

Administrators of small social-service agencies should realize that, when life-change stress is high, special care should be taken to ensure adequate rest. They should postpone important decisions and avoid dealing with policy "shoot-outs" with superiors until stresses have subsided.

The Last One in the Box. Species of laboratory animals differ from one another. Hamsters bite and are generally disagreeable. Mice bite also, and they fight among themselves. Guinea pigs, however, docilely accept their fate and seem to love their handlers. Occasionally, scientists have to kill a number of guinea pigs in order to obtain certain tissues or fluids for research purposes. As 15 or 20 pigs are removed from a box one by one, you can imagine the remaining pigs saying "Where is Agatha? She's been gone a long time. Herschel still isn't back. What are those frightening sounds coming from the other side of the room? What will become of us?" The guinea pigs crowd together in the box. They rub against one another to draw comfort and strength. The last two pigs huddle together as the group did. When only one pig remains, it is shaking, frightened, *biting,* and nervous.

In this respect, humans are not unlike guinea pigs. We are often afraid of change, failure, illness, and death. When these events occur, it sometimes seems as though we are the "last one in the box." No one understands us anymore. No one cares about us. We end up sentencing ourselves to solitary confinement.

When administrators assume new responsibilities, they frequently report a feeling of isolation and estrangement. Excessive change, seemingly thrust upon us, can be especially debilitating during a period of isolation. Each of us can recall a time when we felt like the last one in the box—when we felt that, even if we tried to express our feelings, others wouldn't understand. Such feelings are often associated with geographical relocations, changes in relationships, and career changes. (Notice that the five most serious life-change events, according to Holmes, involve the loss of relationships by one means or another.)

Try to remember a period of isolation in your life. What did you do to help yourself? Because of the variety of feelings associated with isolation—hopelessness, depression, and hostility—you may have tried many things before you found a solution.

1.   Describe a last-one-in-the-box experience in your life. It may have been intensely painful or only mildly disturbing. How did you feel? Be specific.
2.   What did you do to try to escape from your box? Be specific.
3.   What happened? What did you do to move past this painful experience? Be specific.

Tentative results of research we are conducting show that emergence from isolation usually involves another person or persons. It is seldom the result of a two-week diet of brown rice, or lifting weights, or medication. It may be a chance telephone call, or contact with a stranger. The "hole in your box" was probably a person.

I have discovered that, for most of us, "high-cost situations" exist when one or more basic need is unmet. Each of us needs to feel good about ourselves—to feel worthy and able. We also need to feel connected with others and prized for our uniqueness without sacrificing that connection. If you find that these needs are being met in your daily activities, I assume you are happy. If you feel that these needs aren't being met, costs may be high for you just now.

THE ABILITY TO TEST ALLEGED LIMITATIONS
BY TAKING ACTION

Most of us underestimate our abilities. The only way in which we can discover our real limitations—intellectual, physical, and emotional—is to test ourselves. We may have been taught to be passive (to be "nice") even though we pay the price by bottling up anger, remaining unassertive, and experiencing depression. We continue to tolerate conflicts while we consume antacid tablets, use alcohol to excess, and desperately search for new employment.

We sometimes tolerate high-cost/low-benefit situations because we're waiting for others—superiors, peers, or employees—to give us permission to change our situation. But we can test our *own* limits simply by taking action. Your idea for a new project is unsound? Who says so? Try it! You aren't the person to prepare and deliver public-service announcements? Who says so? Prove them wrong by doing an excellent job in your own way. You haven't enough experience to lobby for increased funding for your agency? Who says so? Try it! You can't find the time to pursue further academic study? Really? Try it!

The Pipe of Oughts and Shoulds. Many of us urgently need to reexamine the adjustment demands that control our lives. We often seem to move through what might be termed a *pipe of oughts and shoulds.* For example, administrators might feel they ought to work 18 hours per day, be socially active, expand agency services, develop an independent consulting service, be the perfect model for staff members, and always appear supremely capable. They might be caught in a "pipe" of impossibly demanding, narrowly defined oughts and shoulds.

People who find that their "pipe" is killing them, both emotionally and physically, often hesitate to change their schedules for fear of being labeled *lazy, irresponsible,* or *incapable:* they go on until a disaster occurs.

If we dare to admit that we would prefer a less stressful, more personally rewarding role, we probably wouldn't receive a very enthusiastic response. In fact, in our culture, there are only a few socially acceptable ways in which we can leave the "pipe." Some of the more popular ways of gaining permission to leave are to suffer a nervous breakdown, a bleeding ulcer, or a heart attack. Following one of these unfortuante "mishaps," those who are closest to us will give us permission to change our life-style.

We can leave our pipes if we decide that the costs are too high. We can choose other life-styles with different combinations of costs and benefits. We might have to give up a great deal in order to make the change, but, after all, physical and emotional survival is at stake.

1. List the five most demanding oughts and shoulds in your life and the costs associated with them.
2. Indicate how you would like to change these oughts and shoulds.
3. How do you cope with high stress? What do you do?
4. In your opinion, what will be the result of your present coping style?
5. How would you like to be able to deal with stress?
6. Why don't you do that?

THE ABILITY TO ASSUME RESPONSIBILITY FOR DESIGNING YOUR OWN LIFE-STYLE

Thrivers take pride in designing their own professional and personal life-styles. There are many alternative life-styles and value systems to choose from in our contemporary society. Marriage is no longer required as a condition of social acceptance. Great wealth does not grant an automatic title of honor. There is a growing feeling that status should be measured by the *quality* of one's life and that helping should be a valued unit of exchange.

I'm not suggesting that we are or should be without constraints. You can dress as you wish, for example, except for those specific occasions—budget hearings and advisory board meetings—on which it is best that you wear a proper "uniform." A compromise? Yes, but an insignificant one when you realize that one of the richest rewards of administering social-service agencies is the fact that real human values and concerns are at issue.

"Letting the Crazies Out." I always hear interesting replies when I ask groups and individuals what they would do if they were allowed to lose control, or freak out. What would *you* do if stresses were overwhelming and you no longer cared what people thought about your behavior? Would you bite people on their ankles, scream, paint graffiti on office buildings, have the worst temper tantrum in the history of civilization? What would you do?

Healthy persons are usually able to find appropriate ways of letting their crazies out. Although a full-blown crazy might involve a permanent and abrupt move to Pago Pago, a minicrazy might involve a weekend at the beach. The point is, when people are unable to release their frustrations in appropriate ways, they eventually pay an exorbitant emotional price.

SUMMARY

Each of us is ultimately responsible for meeting our survival needs. We cannot expect supervisors, boards of directors, or staff members to give us the help we need. We need to assert ourselves in productive ways.

If we fail to practice the choosing skills—if we refuse to explore our alternatives—we can be led to feel as though we're trapped in a dead-end situation. Active choosers live professional and personal lives characterized by forward momentum.

When personal emotional costs escalate, we need to adapt by reexamining our choices instead of grimly setting ourselves up for physical and emotional illness.

When we give ourselves permission to test ourselves—to try new ventures—both professionally and personally, we adopt a growth posture. Tasks we once felt were impossible are accomplished. People who inadvertently hurt us are taught to respect us in new ways.

Finally, the search for our own unique life-style is a continuous process of challenges, failures, and successes.

SUGGESTED REFERENCES

Alberti, R. E., & Emmons, M. L. *Your perfect right.* San Luis Obispo, Calif.: Impact, 1974. Alberti and Emmons explore the significance of nonassertive, aggressive, and assertive behavior patterns for individual and collective health. The book includes an excellent annotated bibliography, extensive lists of references, and an Assertiveness Inventory.

Corey, G., & Corey, M. S. *Groups: Process and practice.* Monterey, Calif.: Brooks/Cole, 1977. Two experienced group leaders, members of a husband-and-wife team, describe the basic issues and key concepts of group process, and show how leaders can apply these concepts in working with a wide range of groups in many settings. This is a theory-based, how-to-do-it book.

Dahms, A. *Thriving: beyond adjustment.* Monterey, Calif.: Brooks/Cole, 1980. An exploration of four central thriving skills cast against a background of the human age span. Discussions of Eastern thought and futurists' predictions are included as well as practical exercises.

Fensterheim, H., & Baer, J. *Don't say yes when you want to say no.* New York: Dell, 1975. A helpful collection of exercises and how-to-do-it prescriptions based on behavior therapy. The skills needed to establish and maintain positive interpersonal relationships are described.

Greenwald, J. *Be the person you were meant to be.* New York: Dell, 1975. Drawing on the tenents of Gestalt therapy, the author encourages the reader to minimize unnatural (toxic) behaviors in relating to self and others and to emphasize the discovery of natural (nourishing) attitudes and behaviors. The discussion of how we self-induce toxic behavior is especially intriguing. Antidotes to toxic behavior are described.

Holmes, T. H., & Rahe, R. H. The social readjustment rating scale. *Journal of Psychosomatic Research,* 1967, *11,* 213-218. In this first appearance of the scale in the professional literature, the authors describe how life-change events were ranked. The occurrence of each event evoked or was associated with some adaptive behavior on the part of involved individuals. The scale includes 43 life events common to the experience of most people.

Lakein, A. *How to get control of your time and your life.* New York: Signet Books, 1974. This is an inexpensive paperback that is a very useful basis for staff discussions focusing on ways to use time efficiently and effectively. The author encourages readers to ask themselves three questions: "What are my lifetime goals? How would I like to spend the next three to five years? How would I live my life if I had only six months to live?" Priorities, both professional and personal, flow from these questions and may influence decisions on a daily basis.

Newman, M., & Berkowitz, B. *How to be your own best friend.* New York: Ballantine Books, 1974. The authors respond to questions as if the queries were being put to them by the reader. They explain why we shrink from exploring more satisfying ways of being and discuss the need to take charge by retaining rights for ourselves.

Pfeiffer, J. W., & Jones, J. E. *A handbook of structured experiences for human relations training* (Vol. 1, Rev. ed.). La Jolla, Calif.: University Associates, 1974. This first volume in a multivolume series contains 23 small-group exercises for use in human-relations training. A questionnaire is included that is very useful in assessing staff attitudes concerning group experiences. These and other materials are available from University Associates, 7596 Eads Avenue, La Jolla, California 92037.

Simon, S. B., Howe, L. W., & Kirschenbaum, H. *Values clarification.* New York: Hart Publishing Co., Inc., 1972. This book illustrates the seven subprocesses of valuing: (1) prizing and cherishing, (2) publicly affirming, when appropriate, (3) choosing from alternatives, (4) choosing after considering consequences, (5) choosing freely, (6) acting, and (7) acting consistently. The book contains 79 exercises that require active choosing among alternatives in ways that reveal and clarify values.

Slater, P. *The pursuit of loneliness.* Boston: Beacon Press, 1970. Slater identifies pressures in modern society that lead to the lack of personal fulfillment. He includes a disturbing analysis of our tendency to "throw away" citizens who do not meet arbitrary standards.

Smith, J. J. *When I say no, I feel guilty.* New York: Bantam Books, 1975. Smith describes the theory and practice of systematic assertive therapy. The book contains a rich collection of situations and recommended coping techniques. A list of suggested technical readings is included.

AFTERWORD

This book grew from our realization that good intentions do not ensure success. Administrative skills must be combined with a genuine commitment to the helping process if positive agency activities are to result. We hope that you've found this book valuable. We hope that you now feel more capable of planning and evaluating funding proposals, discovering new communication skills, managing volunteer programs, and dealing effectively with conflict situations.

We regret that we cannot know the special conditions in which you're working—those unique pressures you're confronting. We believe the ideas presented here can be applied in any setting, and we're confident that you will achieve your personal and professional goals.

We wish that we could meet you. As an alternative, we invite you to contact us at the address below. We're especially interested in the techniques you've discovered. Moreover, we would like to hear your reactions to this book.

Accept our best wishes for personal and professional success as an administrative leader committed to meeting human needs at the grassroots level.

Brooks/Cole Publishing Company
555 Abrego St.
Monterey, CA   93940

APPENDIX A
BIBLIOGRAPHY

Since the administration of community services has not yet been recognized as a professional discipline, there are virtually no books available that relate directly to the broad spectrum of skills and knowledge necessary to be effective and useful at this level of administration. The books listed in this bibliography range from philosophical discourses to very basic "how to" publications.

Alinsky, S. D. *Rules for radicals.* New York: Random House, 1971.

Alinsky, S. D. *Reveille for radicals.* New York: Vintage, 1969.

Bernstein, I. H., & Freeman, H. E. *Academic and entrepreneurial research.* New York: Russell Sage, 1975.

Bolles, R. *What color is your parachute?* Berkeley, Calif.: Ten Speed Press, 1974.

Brown, S. W., Jr. *Storefront organizing.* New York: Pyramid, 1972.

Caiden, G. E. *The dynamics of public administration.* Hinsdale, Ill. Dryden Press, 1971.

Caro, F. (Ed.). *Readings in evaluation research.* New York: Russell Sage, 1971.

Church, D. M. *How to succeed with volunteers.* New York: National Public Relations Council of Health & Welfare Services, 1962.

Cloward, R. A., & Piven, F. F. *Regulating the poor: The functions of public welfare.* New York: Vintage, 1971.

Coleman, J. S. *Community conflict.* New York: Free Press, 1957.

Conrad, W. R., & Glenn, W. R. *The effective voluntary board of directors.* Chicago: Swallow Press, 1976.

Cornuelle, R. *De-managing America—The final revolution.* New York: Bantam, 1977.

Coser, L. *Continuities in the study of social conflict.* New York: Free Press, 1967.

Drucker, P. F. *The practice of management.* New York: Harper & Row, 1954.

Drucker, P. F. *Management: Tasks, responsibilities, practices.* New York: Harper & Row, 1974.

Duley, J. *Implementing field experience education.* San Francisco: Jossey-Bass, 1974.

Flesch, R. *The art of plain talk.* New York: Collier, 1951.

Gardner, J. W. *Self-renewal: The individual and the innovative society.* New York: Harper & Row, 1964.

Gardner, J. W. *Excellence.* New York: Harper & Row, 1961.

Guttentag, M., & Struening, E. L. (Eds.). *Handbook of evaluation research.* Beverly Hills, Calif.: Sage, 1975.

Hardy, J. M. *Corporate planning for nonprofit organizations.* New York: Association Press, 1972.

Hasenfeld, Y., & English, R. A. *Human service organizations.* Ann Arbor: University of Michigan Press, 1974.

Hillman, H., & Abarbanel, K. *The art of winning foundation grants.* New York: Vanguard, 1975.

Houle, C. O. *The effective board.* New York: Association Press, 1960.

Hull, R., & Peter, L. J. *The Peter principle.* New York: Bantam, 1972.

Illich, I. *Deschooling society.* New York: Harrow Books, 1970.

Keaton, M. T., & Associates. *Experiential learning.* San Francisco: Jossey-Bass, 1976.

Krathwohl, D. *How to prepare a research proposal.* New York: Syracuse University Press, 1966.

Kredenser, G. *Write it right!* New York: Barnes and Noble, 1972.

Litwin, G. H., & Stringer, A., Jr. *Motivation and organizational climate.* Cambridge, Mass.: Harvard University Press, 1968.

Mackenzie, A. R. *The time trap.* New York: McGraw-Hill, 1972.

Mager, R. F. *Goal analysis and preparing instructional objectives.* New York: Siegler-Fearon, 1972.

McLuhan, M. and Fiore, Q. *The medium is the message: An inventory of effect.* New York: Bantam Books, 1967.

McLaughlin, F. (Ed.). *The mediate teacher.* North American Publishing, 1975.

Meyer, P. *Awarding college credit for non-college learning.* San Francisco: Jossey-Bass, 1975.

Naylor, H. H. *Volunteers today.* Dryden Associates, 1973.

Nash, K. *Get the best of yourself.* New York: Grosset and Dunlap, 1976.

O. M. Collective. *The organizer's manual.* New York: Bantam, 1977.

Parkinson, N. C. *Parkinson's law.* New York: Ballantine, 1957.

Pifer, A. The jeopardy of private institutions. *Annual report for 1970/The report of the President.* New York: Carnegie, 1970.

Schindler-Rainman, E. & Lippitt, R. *The volunteer community: Creative use of human resources.* Fairfax, Va.: NTL/Learning Resources, 1975.

Ringer, R. J. *Winning through intimidation.* New York: Fawcett, 1974.

Schumacher, E. F. *Small is beautiful.* New York: Perennial Library, 1973.

Seymour, H. J. *Designs for fund-raising.* New York: McGraw-Hill, 1966.

Shefter, H. *Short cuts to effective English.* New York: Pocket Books, 1976.

Strunk, W., Jr., & White, E. B. *The elements of style.* New York: Macmillan, 1972.

Suchman, E. A. *Evaluative research: Principles and practice in public service and social action programs.* New York: Russell Sage, 1967.

Tocqueville, A. de. *Democracy in America.* New York: Vintage Books, 1955.

Toffler, A. *Future shock.* New York: Bantam, 1971.

Townsend, R. *Up the organization.* New York: Fawcett, 1970.

Trecker, H. B. *Social work administration.* New Your: Association Press, 1971.

Weiss, C. H. *Evaluation research: Methods of assessing program effectiveness.*
   Englewood Cliffs, N. J.: Prentice-Hall, 1972.
Wilson, M. *The effective management of volunteer programs.* Boulder, Colo.:
   Volunteer Management Associates, 1976.

APPENDIX B

PRIMARY SOURCES OF FOUNDATION PUBLICATIONS

The Foundation Center is a nonprofit organization located in New York City. The publications listed below can be obtained from the Foundation Center or from major libraries. The address and telephone number of the Foundation Center is: 888 Seventh Avenue, New York, New York 10019, (212) 975-1120.

The Foundation Directory (6th ed.)
Marianna O. Lewis, Editor
September 1977, 650 Pages
Introduction by Thomas R. Buckman

The Foundation Directory is the most important reference work available on grant-making foundations in the U.S. The sixth edition includes updated information concerning the 2818 largest foundations in the U.S. Each of these foundations has assets of more than $1 million or awards grants in excess of $100,000 annually. Representing total assets of more than $28 billion in 1975/76, these foundations account for approximately 90% of foundation assets and 80% of the grants awarded by foundations in the U.S.

In addition to information concerning 577 foundations that weren't listed in the previous edition, the sixth edition contains important new data in every entry: foundation telephone numbers, grant application procedures, and frequency of board meetings. The improved subject index lists national and regional foundations. Other useful indexes list foundations according to state and city, foundation donors, trustees and administrators, and foundation names.

The analytical introduction includes statistical tables and compilations that present up-to-date profiles of foundations according to size, location, amounts of grants, and subject interest.

$35 plus $1 postage and handling.

Order from: Columbia University Press
136 South Broadway
Irvington, New York 10533

The Foundation Grants Index
Bimonthly
Included as a separate section in *Foundation News*

The Foundation Grants Index lists currently reported foundation grants of $5000 or more with recipient and key-word subject indexes. Each listing includes the recipient's name and address, the amount and date of the grant, and

179

the grant's purpose (if available). An average bimonthly index lists more than 1600 grant awards, totaling approximately $100 million.

$20 annual subscription rate for *Foundation News.*

Order from: The Council on Foundations, Inc.

                Box 783

                Old Chelsea Station, New York 10011

The Foundation Grants Index, 1976
Annual Volume
Lee Noe, Grants Editor
1977, 361 pages

This is an annual cumulation of the grant information and indexes that appear in *Foundation News*. It includes detailed summaries of about 10,000 grants made by approximately 300 major foundations with a total value exceeding $700 million. It contains representative reports of current grants by large national foundations, providing a valuable guide to their grant-making interests.

$15 plus $1 postage and handling.

Order from: Columbia University Press

                136 South Broadway

                Irvington, New York 10533

The Foundation Center National Data Book
September 1977

This is the only directory that includes information on the more than 27,000 nonprofit organizations in the U.S. that are classified as private foundations by the Internal Revenue Service. A brief profile of each foundation is presented. Listings include foundation names, addresses, principal officers, assets, amounts of grants made, and gifts received in the most recent year of record, which is specified. (Most of the information is taken from 1975 tax returns.)

Two means of access to the profiles are provided. They are listed both alphabetically and by location. This directory is most useful for identifying foundations of a particular size or in a particular area.

For description and price, write to:

                The Foundation Center

                888 Seventh Avenue

                New York, New York 10019

Comsearch Printouts
Annual
1976

Comsearch Printouts contains printouts in 54 subject areas listing 1976 grants by more than 300 major foundations. These listings, which are compiled through computer searches of the Foundation Grants Data Bank, serve as guides to major foundations. The list of categories includes fields in the arts, sciences, and humanities. Under each foundation name in each category are listed all the grants made in that category by the foundation. Grant listings include the names and addresses of the recipients, the size of the grants, and descriptions of the activities that were funded.

Available in microfiche ($3 per subject, prepaid) and paper printout ($11 per subject, prepaid).

Request complete list of available subjects from:
>The Foundation Center
>888 Seventh Avenue
>New York, New York 10019

Foundation Grants to Individuals
August 1977

This publication profiles the programs of more than 1000 foundations that make grants to individuals. The foundations described in this book have made awards to students, artists, scholars, musicians, scientists, and writers. The book contains information concerning sources of funds for scholarships, fellowships, internships, medical and emergency assistance, residencies, and travel grants.

The foundations included represent assets of more than $4 billion. In the most recent year of record, these funding sources awarded grants totaling more than $56 million to over 40,000 individuals.

Each entry includes a foundation's address, the name of the person to whom correspondence should be addressed, the amount of the foundation's assets, the total amount of the grants it has awarded, the portion of the grant total that was awarded to individuals, the number of individuals who have received grants, application information, and a description of the portion of the foundation's program that relates to individuals. A detailed subject index is included.

$12 plus $1 postage and handling, prepaid.
Order from: The Foundation Center
>888 Seventh Avenue
>New York, New York 10019

About Foundations: How to Find the Facts you Need to Get a Grant:
Judith B. Margolin
1977 Revised Edition, 48 pages

This paperback booklet is intended to serve as a guide to conducting foundation-funding research. It includes step-by-step instructions for those who need to obtain information regarding a specific foundation, the names of foundations in a specific area, or a list of foundations interested in funding projects in a specific subject area. Explicit directions are given for the most efficient and thorough usage of standard foundation reference tools, such as foundation annual reports and IRS information returns. Printed and microfiche sources of information are identified and illustrated. The information resources available at The Foundation Center's national and regional library collections are described.

The first edition, which sold out quickly, was used by experienced fund raisers and newcomers to the foundation field. The revised edition updates the original material. The booklet describes important sources of information concerning foundations and provides a list of 33 state and regional foundation directories.

$3 prepaid.

Order from: The Foundation Center
               888 Seventh Avenue
               New York, New York 10019

Foundation Center Source Book Profiles
Annual Looseleaf Subscription Service
August 1977

Analytical profiles of more than 500 foundations are provided to subscribers in the first year. Foundations in the U.S. that award more than $200,000 per year are listed.

Subscribers receive 40 to 45 new profiles every month. Profiles are approximately three to five pages in length. They include a detailed breakdown of grants by subject area (art, education, and so on), by grant type (construction, general support, and so on), and by recipient type (such as private secondary schools or university medical schools). Each foundation's current giving is compared with its historical grant-making pattern and correlated with its overall statement of purpose and activities.

In addition to grant analysis, descriptions contain the names of persons to contact for grant information and complete lists of officers and staff members. An up-to-date analysis contains the amounts of assets, gifts received, and grants awarded. Background information regarding each foundation's founding, donors, and related activities is presented, as are details of application guidelines and procedures. A subject index to the grant-making interests of all profiled foundations is updated every month. Changes in address, personnel, and policy also are updated on a monthly basis.

$150 annual subscription.

Order from: The Foundation Center
               888 Seventh Avenue
               New York, New York 10019

(To obtain information concerning a one-week grantsmanship training program conducted throughout the nation at various times, write: THE GRANTS-MANSHIP CENTER, 1015 West Olympic Boulevard, Los Angeles, California 90015.)

APPENDIX C

GRAPHICS
MADE SIMPLE

"Small community-based, social-service agencies play an important role in bringing needed services to the community. Communication materials that inform, promote, and instruct are crucial to each agency's effectiveness in reaching and serving the public. Since these small agencies often lack the budget for professional consulting and design, the staff itself must fill the gap. In the pages that follow, I have tried to present the basics of good graphic design, which can be developed by the nonprofessional in effectively promoting an agency's image and services."

Pat Kelly has been involved in all aspects of graphic design for the past ten years. She has designed and conducted courses and workshops for staffs and administrators of community-service agencies. She is particularly interested in developing low-cost methods of producing printed and graphic material.

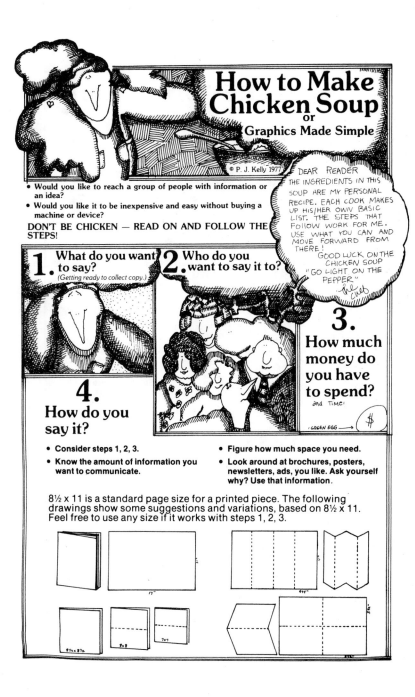

Gather your tools.

Basic Equipment and Materials Needed for Graphic Production with Costs.

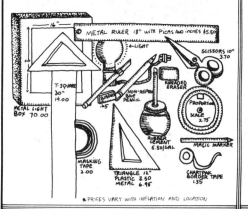

- METAL RULER 18" WITH PICAS AND INCHES $5.50
- SCISSORS 10" 3.70
- 2-LIGHT
- KNEADED ERASER
- T-SQUARE 30" 14.00
- NON-REPRO BLUE PENCIL .65
- BLADE
- METAL LIGHT BOX 70.00
- PROPORTION SCALE 2.75
- RUBBER CEMENT 6.50/GAL.
- MAGIC MARKER
- MASKING TAPE 2.00
- TRIANGLE 12" PLASTIC 3.50 METAL 6.95
- CHARTPAK BORDER TAPE 1.35

*PRICES VARY WITH INFLATION AND LOCATION

6. Make a plan.

- Draw small rough sketches proportionate to final size of printed piece. *(See 6a.)*
- Start with loose shapes that approximate objects in illustrations or photos. *(See 6b.)*
- Make more specific small sketches *(See 6c.)*
- Do a plan for each page if it's a magazine or book.

6. continues . . . .

A **Grid** is a plan that organizes type, copy, photos, and art. A grid also divides space into smaller spaces that are proportionate. The are commonly 2-column, 3-column, and 4-column grid systems.

a.

b.

c.

Spec Type?

(Make sure you give typesetter type-written error-free copy. Mistakes cost time and money.)

To **Spec Type** means choosing the size, style, format, and column width your type-written copy will be set in.

Type is a little confusing at first, but don't give up. Type comes in different sizes and styles like clothes and camels. Build up your courage by building up your vocabulary.

The following information will help you communicate with a typesetter.

- **Points** — A measurement used to describe type sizes. Approximately **72 points = 1 inch.** Type is normally used from 6 pts. to 120 pts.

examples:

6 pt. chicken soup
8 pt. chicken soup
10 pt. chicken soup
12 pt. chicken soup
14 pt. chicken soup
16 pt. chicken soup
18 pt. chicken soup
20 pt. chicken sou
24 pt. chicken s
36 pt. chic
120

- **Pica** *(pi-ca)* — A unit measurement used to describe line lengths. **6 picas = 1 inch.**

72 PTS OR 1 INCH

Conversion Table	Inches	Points	Picas
	1/8	9	3/4
	1/4	18	1 1/2
	3/8	27	2 1/4
	1/2	36	3
	5/8	45	3 3/4
	3/4	54	4 1/2
	7/8	63	5 1/4
	1	72	6

7. continues .... **Words** ....

● **Leading** *(led'ing)* — Space between lines. This is measured in points.

Chicken soup is good tasting any day of the year. Chicken soup is good tasting any day of the year.

EXAMPLES

$\frac{7}{2}$ (1/2 PT LEADING) WITH 9 PT TYPE

Chicken soup is good tasting any day of the year. Chicken soup is good tasting any day of the year.

$\frac{9}{12}$ (2 PT LEADING) WITH 9 PT TYPE

● **Justify** — To space out type lines so that they align in both right and left margins. **Justify right** means type is aligned only right. **Justify left** means type is aligned only left.

SPECIFY All THESE TO TYPESETTER WHEN DESCRIBING YOUR JOB!

● **Ragged** — Describes lines of type that aren't justified.

● **Body Copy** — Type used in the main text portion of the copy. Usually 6 to 14 pt. sizes.

● **Display Type** — Also called Headlines usually is larger type. Gives a brief description or slogan.

SAVE

Copyfitting

is the process to measure the amount of space your typewritten copy will fit into when set in type. To fit copy you need 3 things:

1. The number of characters *(every space, letter, punctuation mark is a character)* per inch or pica in typewritten copy.

2. The number of characters per inch or pica in the typestyle being set.

3. The size of the area to be filled.

The above ingredients all make a good soup. →

Select the paper.
Paper has weight, grade, color, kind. (Consider all these.)

Picas Inches

Picas	Inches
1	
2	
3	
4	
5	
6	1
7	
8	
9	
10	
11	
12	2
13	
14	
15	
16	
17	
18	3
19	
20	
21	
22	
23	
24	4
25	
26	
27	
28	
29	
30	5
31	
32	
33	
34	
35	
36	6
37	
38	
39	
40	
41	
42	7
43	
44	
45	
46	
47	
48	8

Select the color ink from a PMS Book. You can buy this book at your local art store or look at your printer's.

Printers have paper samples. They'll be glad to help you select paper stock. You can also call your local paper distributors.

9. Select a Printer!
(Thought I forgot, didn't you?)

Be sure to give your printer as many details about your job as possible. You may be trying to make Bouillabaisse on a bean soup budget. Time depends on the job. However, try to allow 14 working days at least from delivery to completion of job.

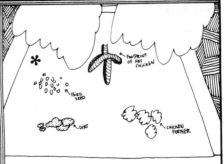

10. Do a pasteup .

If you start with dirt, birdseed, chicken feathers and footprints, that's what you'll end up with.

✱ *These ingredients don't make a good pasteup or a good soup.*

Do a pasteup?

To Start

- **Go back and read step 5.**
- **Gather your tools from an art or drafting supply store.**
- **Be accurate, keep using your T-square to realign and recheck for straightness.**
- **Remember, mistakes in print don't vanish as in the electronic media.**

a.

Need good straight edge, working surface, equipment and light.

→

b.

Use straight edge to align paper.

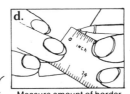

d.

Measure amount of border space desired along paper edge.

←

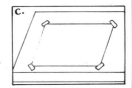

c.

Tape final size of pasteup straight on table. Line up with T-square.

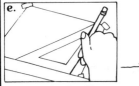

e.

Draw a straight line. The amount of measured border. Use non-repro blue pencil to draw line.(non-repro doesn't photograph on a stat camera)

→

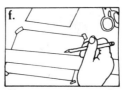

f.

Use non-repro blue pencil for placement of type, photos, folds. Grid is included in this.

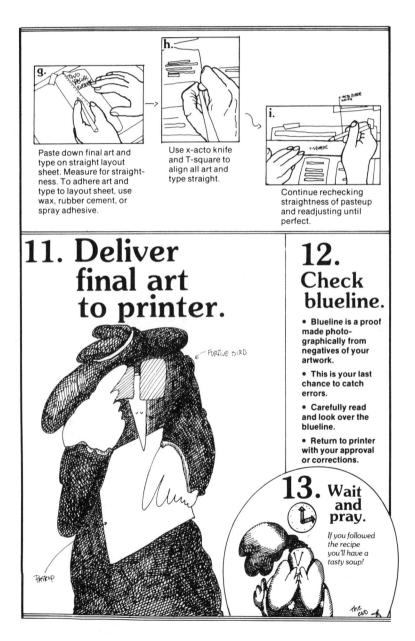

g. Paste down final art and type on straight layout sheet. Measure for straightness. To adhere art and type to layout sheet, use wax, rubber cement, or spray adhesive.

h. Use x-acto knife and T-square to align all art and type straight.

i. Continue rechecking straightness of pasteup and readjusting until perfect.

11. Deliver final art to printer.

12. Check blueline.

- Blueline is a proof made photographically from negatives of your artwork.

- This is your last chance to catch errors.

- Carefully read and look over the blueline.

- Return to printer with your approval or corrections.

13. Wait and pray.

If you followed the recipe you'll have a tasty soup!

INDEX

Abstract, of proposal, 20
Accountability, 29 (*see also* Evaluation)
Action, taking, 169-170
Action plans, 145-147
Administrators, 6-7 (*see also* Leadership)
Advertising, 90-91, 102 (*see also* Press releases)
Advocacy functions, 4-5
Agencies (*see* Community-based social-service agencies)
Alexander, M., 66
Assessment (*see* Evaluation)

Behavior patterns, 156-157
Benz, L., 142
Berry, K. L., 7-8
Bike rides, fund raising, 45
Bingo, as fund raiser, 43
Blake, R., 157, 158
Boards of directors (*see* Governing boards)
Booklets, writing, 71, 82
Brainstorming, 16, 145-146
Bring-your-address-book day (BYAB), 45
Broadcast media, 102-107
Brokering role, 5
Budgets, 5-6, 17, 21-23, 35, 129 (*see also* Funding sources)
Bulletins, writing, 71, 82
Businesses, funding from, 18

Categorizing, of people, 165
Cavanaugh, J., 14
Choosing skills, 164-165
Clientele, 7-8

Clifton, B., 124
Communication (*see also* Writing):
 broadcast media for, 102-107
 channels of, 100-107
 of goals, 28-29
 newsletters for, 87-95
 newspapers for, 100-102
Community-based social-service agencies, 2-9
Community representation, on governing boards, 125-126
Complex individual behavior, 157
Conflict resolution, 142, 143-148, 163
Corporations, funding from, 18
Cost accounting, personal, 165-166, 169-170
Counseling services, 4-5
Country-club management, 158
Crazies, letting out the, 170-171
Crisis aid, 4-5
Cultural environments, 154-155

Dahms, A., 162
Denver Metropolitan Area, 3
Direct-mail technique, fund raising with, 38-40
Dollar-day programs, 45
Drucker, P., 116

Educational services/programs, 4
Ego involvement, 18
Eisenman, A. G., 86
Emotional survival, 163-173
Employment services, 4
Evaluation, 49-62
 analysis and feedback of, 59-60
 approaches to, 52, 53

Evaluation (continued)
  conflict resolution and, 144, 147
  cost of, 60-61
  data gathering methods for, 57-59
  elements of, 56-60
  of goal achievement, 28, 29
  implementation procedures,
    after, 60
  models of, 54-55
  in proposal, 21
  purposes of, 51
  questions posed during, 56-57
  research design for, 55-56
  on site, 53-54
  timing of, 52
  types of, 52
  of volunteer programs, 121-122
External influences, 153-156

Foundations, funding from, 18,
    179-183
Fund raising, 35-46
  of large contributions, 37-38, 44
  of medium contributions, 38-40
  planning and research in, 35-37
  presentations, 42
  of small contributions, 40
Funding sources, 5-6, 15
  identifying, 36-37
  meetings with, 19
  in private sector, 18
  in public sector, 18-19
  writing formal proposal to, 19-21

Garage sales, fund raising, 41
Goals, 27-32, 155
  agency compared with project,
    29-30
  of conflict resolution, 145
  necessity of, 28-29
  planning process and, 116-118
  procedures to implement, 30-31
  writing statement of, 31-32
Governing boards, 125-130
Graphics, basics of good, 184-191

Handy, C. B., 154
Higgins, K., 152
Holmes, T. H., 166-167

Impact evaluation, 52
Impoverished management, 157
In-kind contributions, 44
Influence, 153-155 (see also
    Leadership)
Informal reports, 68-73
Internal influences, 153
Isolation, feelings of, 168-169
Issues, policy, 127-128

Job placement/training services, 4
Jones, B., 48

Kelly, P., 184

Las Vegas-Night events, 43
"Last-one-in-the-box" feeling,
    168-169
Leadership, styles of, 156-158
Legal aspects, of governing boards,
    129
Legislators, approaching, 137, 138
Letters:
  as reports, 70, 82
  of transmittal, 80
Life-change stress, 166-167
Life-style, designing own, 170-171
Limitations, testing alleged, 169-170
Lindblom, K., 26
Line-item budgets, 21, 22-23
Lobbying process, 135-140
Lunches, fund raising, 42

McLean, C., 134
McLuhan, M., 73
Management-by-objective (MBO),
    27, 28
Management, styles of, 157-158
Maslow, A., 157
Media events, 103
Memoranda, 69-70, 82

Methods, statement of, 21
Middle-of-the-road management, 157
Miniproposals, 40-41
Minutes, writing, 71-72, 82
Monitoring approach, to evaluation,
    51
Morale, bad, 145
Mouton, J., 157, 158
Movies, fund raising, 44

Needs:
    agency's statement of, 17, 20
    individual's hierarchy of, 157
Newsletters, 87-95
    advertising in, 90-91
    building circulation of, 93-94
    editing news briefs for, 91-92
    evaluation of, 94
    fund raising with, 43
    lay out and paste up of, 89-90
    major news stories for, 92-93
    materials needed to produce,
        88
    place fillers in, 93
    producing, 88-89
    proofreading final copy for, 93
    purposes of, 87
Newspapers, communication with,
    100-102
Nicoletti, J., 142

Objectives, program, 17, 20-21,
    27-28 (see also Goals)
Open houses, fund raising, 42-43
Oughts/shoulds, 169-170
Outcome evaluation, 52
Outreach programs, 4-5

People-oriented agencies, 155
Personal-sharing functions, 5
Planning process, 116-117, 127-128
Policy, planning, 127-128
Political activity, of lobbying,
    135-140
Power-oriented agencies, 154
Press releases, 100-102

Price, W., 127
Procedures:
    definitions of, 28-29, 30-31
    writing statement of, 31-32
Process evaluation, 52
Program and resource development,
    14-24 (see also Funding
    sources):
    basic concepts of, 15
    stages in, 16-24
Project-goal statement, 30
Public-service announcements
    (PSAS), 103-107
Publicity, 99-108

Quality-of-life supplements, 4

Radio, public-service announcements
    on, 103, 104-105
Raismus, J. de, 129
Rational-economic behavior, 156
Referral services, 2, 4
Relationships, choosing, 165
Reports:
    formalizing sections of, 79-80
    writing, 68-73
Resources (see Budgets; Fund raising;
    Funding sources; Program and
    resource development)
Role-oriented agencies, 155
Runs, fund raising, 45

Sales, fundraising, 44
Schierling, D., 34
Schmidt, W. H., 158
Self-actualizing behavior, 157
Services, 2-5
Short reports, writing, 73, 82
Shoulds/oughts, 169-170
Slater, P., 165
Social-change approach, to
    evaluation, 51
Social individual behavior, 156
Social Readjustment Rating Scale,
    166-167